THE REGENCY

THE
REGENCY

JOANNA RICHARDSON

COLLINS

ST JAMES'S PLACE, LONDON

The publishers wish to thank the following for the illustrations used in this book.

John W. R. Barrow, 111; *Brighton Corporation*, 48, 65; *Mary Evans*, 20, 23(b), 92; *John Freeman*, 7, 22, 25, 27, 28, 29, 30, 34, 35 (both), 40, 41 (all), 49, 50(b), 55, 56 (all), 58 (all), 73(b), 74 (both), 76 (both), 77, 80, 81, 88 (both), 97(a), 99, 107, 109, 113, 139; *The Mansell Collection*, 32, 36, 45, 46 (both), 50(a), 61, 63 (both), 71, 72, 73(a), 82, 84, 87, 90, 91, 93, 96, 97(b), 98, 104, 108, 112, 127, 131; *The National Portrait Gallery*, 31, 42(b), 100, 101, 115, 116, 117, 125, 128; *The Radio Times Hulton Picture Library*, 8, 9, 10, 11 (both), 15, 23(a), 39, 44, 52, 60, 62, 66, 68, 69, 78, 85, 95, 105, 110, 121, 129, 134; *Edwin Smith*, 64, 67; *The Tate Gallery*, 106; *Victoria & Albert Museum*, 83, 103.

First published 1973
© Joanna Richardson 1973

ISBN 0 00 192290 4

Made and printed in Great Britain by
William Collins Sons & Co Ltd Glasgow

CONTENTS

FOR
SIMON AND SARAH
WITH LOVE

I. THE PRINCE REGENT

On Wednesday, 6th February, 1811, before the Privy Council, George Augustus Frederick, Prince of Wales, was sworn in as Prince Regent of the United Kingdom. On Saturday, 29th January, 1820, "without any appearance of pain and without a lucid interval", in the 82nd year of his life, after a reign of 59¼ years, King George III died at Windsor. Between these two events lay the Regency. For the first time in history, an English sovereign had been recognised as mentally deranged, and his eldest son had been appointed to rule in his stead. This historical phenomenon lasted for nine years: nine years distinguished in literature and the arts – among them the art of living – famous in science, memorable in politics and war. The spirit of those years, the Regency, was the spirit of the Regent himself. Patriot, scholar, sportsman, patron of the arts and man of fashion, arbiter of taste, he was the most accomplished man of his age and the most gifted ruler of England since Charles I.

He had been born on 12th August, 1762, the first child of George III and his plain and elegant wife, Charlotte of Mecklenburg-Strelitz. On the fifth day after his birth he was created Prince of Wales. Three years later he was made a Knight of the Garter. But his childhood was not simply a record of pomp and circumstance. He was looked after, as a biographer wrote, "with unexampled

7

Kew Palace, birthplace of the Prince of Wales. Life at Kew was domestic
and delightfully rural: the royal children learned to sow and harvest the
wheat from which they also made their own bread.

care". His parents were delightfully domestic, and, despite their
royalty, there remained an idyllic quality about life in the palace at
Kew. The older children were taught by a governess and sub-
governess, and the Prince of Wales and his brother Frederick, Duke
of York, later moved to a separate house with their tutors. As small
boys, they were given a practical lesson in agriculture: they dug a
plot of ground, sowed it with wheat, harvested the crop, winnowed
it, and baked their own loaves of bread. The King and Queen ate
the bread with them, "and beheld with pleasure the very amusements
of their children rendered the source of useful knowledge".

They were given not only useful knowledge, but a taste for the
arts. The establishment at Kew included Johann Christian Bach,
the composer's youngest son, who was music master in the Queen's
household. As a young child, the Prince of Wales went to Covent
Garden to see *The Fairy Favour*, a children's operetta with music by
J. C. Bach. It was specially performed in his honour. He was also
made aware of the world of painting; for that elegant artist John
Zoffany was commissioned to portray the Prince of Wales and the

Duke of York as cupids. Unfortunately the picture has vanished, but two other paintings by Zoffany record the Prince's childhood. One shows him in the park at Windsor, with his mother and her brothers from Mecklenburg-Strelitz; the other shows him with his sister, the Princess Royal, in Queen Charlotte's dressing-room in old Buckingham House. The Prince is wearing Roman military costume, and the Princess is dressed in oriental style. Thomas Gainsborough, who was also commissioned to paint the royal children, found them "a constellation of youthful beauty".

In 1771, when the Prince was nine, and the Duke of York was eight, Dr William Markham was appointed their tutor. Dean of Christ Church, Oxford, and Bishop of Chester, Dr Markham also found time to supervise his royal charges at Kew. No doubt the Prince of Wales owed much of his taste for the classics to this much-loved friend. By 1780, when he came of age, he was a classical scholar and a fluent speaker of French, Italian and German. He had formed sound literary tastes, he was an accomplished amateur singer, he had an appreciation of the fine arts. He could draw, he could play the violoncello, and he could fence. But, alas, his education was sadly

George III, Queen Charlotte, and their children, by John Zoffany

9

The Prince of Wales and the Princess Royal with Queen Charlotte in her dressing-room, by John Zoffany. The Prince is wearing Roman military costume, his sister is dressed in Oriental style.

deficient. He had been kept in ignorance of social conditions: completely ignorant of the vast world that lay beyond Kew Palace. Though he was heir to the Throne of England, no one had tried to form his character. No one had clearly shown him the difference between right and wrong.

When, at last, he came of age, the Prince enjoyed all the pleasures he had not known. But he did not spend his time entirely in revelry. He sat again to Gainsborough (he sat for him nine times in all), he sat to Sir Joshua Reynolds, and he attended the Royal Academy dinner, where they were all delighted with him. He had already begun to show himself a patron of the arts. In 1783 he fell in love with a little fishing village on the coast of Sussex which was still sometimes known as Brighthelmstone. The following year he bought a substantial farmhouse there, with an unbroken view of the sea, and in 1785 he employed the architect Henry Holland to enlarge it. The elegant two-storey house, with its bow-fronted rooms, was to influence local architecture for half a century. But it was not the Pavilion which the Prince would leave to posterity.

However, by the time he found the farmhouse at Brighton, he had already installed himself in the London palace which would be the

Top: the fishing village of Brighthelmstone, later known as Brighton. The Prince bought a farmhouse there in 1784. Above: by 1804 Brighton had a royal elegance. The Prince is shown riding, with the Steyne and the Pavilion in the background.

Nonesuch of the age. When he reached his twenty-first birthday, the King had given him Carlton House. It stood on the site of the present Waterloo Place, with handsome gardens stretching down to the Mall. It needed considerable repair and decoration, and it offered him a breathtaking chance to create a brave new world that would reflect his taste, his dignity, his love of pleasure and splendour. Henry Holland set to work on it. In 1784, when the interior was finished, the Prince gave a grand ball "to the principal nobility and gentry". This was followed, two months later, by a public breakfast.

As a chronicler recorded: "About six hundred persons assembled in the gardens at two o'clock. The preparations were very magnificent: covers were laid under nine marquees for two hundred and fifty persons; and the refreshments consisted of the finest fruits of the season, confectionaries, ices, creams, and ornamental designs. After the company had taken refreshments, they rose to dance . . ."

"You cannot call it magnificent," Horace Walpole wrote of Carlton House. "It is the taste and propriety that strike . . . You never was in so pretty a scene." Walpole – no mean judge of style – thought that Carlton House would be the most perfect palace in Europe.

Distinguished men, accustomed to splendour, fine manners and fine intellects, did not merely admire Carlton House, they admired the Prince who created it. William Beckford, the author and socialite, and the builder of Fonthill, the gigantic Gothic abbey near Salisbury, declared that the Prince was "brighter than sunshine, and cast a brilliant gleam wherever he moved". Joseph Haydn, the composer, decided that "the Prince of Wales is the most handsome man on God's earth". Antonio Canova, the Italian sculptor, extolled his "fine taste, sound judgment, and extensive information" about the arts. He also observed, when the Prince was King, "that he knew no Sovereign in whose address were more happily combined, the suavity of the amicable man, and the dignity of the great Monarch."

Even now, when he came of age, the Prince knew more than most of his contemporaries about the art of living. He was constantly learning – and constantly showing his many interests. He attended the ceremony held to commemorate the anniversary of the death of Handel. He played in quartets at Carlton House. He hunted stags at Windsor, though sometimes the stag was taken after a run of thirty or even forty miles. He summoned Henry Angelo, the famous fencing master, to give an exhibition of his skill. At Covent Garden

he asked his friend, the young actor John Philip Kemble, to exchange
a pinch of snuff in the royal box. He was elegant, handsome, gifted,
and his manners were a pleasure to behold.

It was in about 1783 that he first saw Maria Fitzherbert. He was
twenty-one, and she was twenty-seven. Their love for each other was
to be the supreme event in both their lives. "If ever the Prince loved
a woman," wrote a critic, "it was she; and half London, had he
thrown the handkerchief, would have flown to pick it up." Mrs
Fitzherbert came of an old Catholic family. Her first husband, an
elderly widower, had died within a year of their marriage. Her
second husband, Thomas Fitzherbert, had died prematurely of
tuberculosis. Mrs Fitzherbert was now a young widow with a house
near Park Lane. She was not conventionally beautiful, but she was
a woman of exceptional distinction. She was gentle, maternal,
devout, high-principled and endearing, and she loved the Prince
not for his status, but for himself. In 1785 she went through a form
of marriage with him. Had he been simply a peer of the realm, he
might have lived very happily ever after.

However, he was under twenty-five and he had not asked the
King's consent, so the marriage was invalid under the Royal
Marriages Act. He had also chosen to marry a Catholic, and so, by
the Act of Settlement, he would forfeit the Crown. Mrs Fitzherbert
promised to keep the marriage secret; she exacted no conditions,
and she trusted to his honour. She behaved impeccably. "Her own
manners," wrote Mary Frampton, the diarist, "ever remained quiet,
civil and unpretending, and in the days of her greatest influence she
was never accused of using it improperly."

The Prince and Mrs Fitzherbert were painted by Gainsborough
and Cosway. At Brighton the Prince's farmhouse, now transformed
into a pavilion, was habitable in 1787, and in the grounds (since the
marriage could not be acknowledged) rose the elegant house designed by Robert Adam for "Mrs Fitz". In 1788 this delightful
existence was interrupted by the King's first attack of insanity. It
became clear that the Prince of Wales might need to rule for him,
and Parliament – and the public – hotly debated the Regency Bill,
in which the terms of the possible Regency were laid down. It was
to be a Regency with limited powers until the King was considered
permanently incapable of reigning.

In 1789, the cabals and debates proved to be unnecessary. The

King's physicians declared that he had recovered. "The King is recovered, and everybody else, I think, gone mad," wrote Lady Louisa Stuart to Lady Portarlington. "Oh, what a winter have we passed!" London was illuminated to celebrate the King's recovery, and the screen of Carlton House was lighted with flambeaux.

The Prince again enjoyed his life: his racing, hunting and fencing. He showed himself a staunch patron of the ring. He is said to have driven the boxer Tom Spring through the streets of London, and he "frequently shook hands" with the pugilist Tom Cribb. (Cribb was later among the prize fighters, dressed as pages, who kept order at his Coronation.) Long before he became friends with George (Beau) Brummell, the patron of pugilists also showed himself to be the patron of fashion; and if he dared to wear the latest colour, a brilliant blue-grey called Emperor's Eye, if he created extravagant vogues for curled hair and large cravats, he himself became every dress. He designed shoe buckles and lavishly frogged surtouts for himself, and he would one day delight in devising new uniforms for his army. These interests did not show an undue and unmanly concern for trivia: they were facets of his artistic sense.

He welcomed his ability to patronise the arts. He patronised Gainsborough, Reynolds, Romney and Hoppner. He enjoyed the theatre: he showed his admiration for Mrs Siddons, invited Kemble to dinner, and presided when the cornerstone of the new Covent Garden Theatre was laid (he later laid the first stone of the new theatre in Drury Lane). He delighted in music, attended concerts, and accompanied Haydn, "quite tolerably", on the violoncello.

Alas, his way of life had brought him heavily into debt. His father agreed to pay his debts provided that he made an official marriage. On 8th April, 1795, compelled to do so by financial straits, the Prince of Wales married Caroline of Brunswick. The King approved, for she was the daughter of his favourite sister – but it was the most irresponsible marriage in modern English history. The Prince of Wales, above all men, needed a suitable and happy marriage. It is scarcely credible, but he had never set eyes on Caroline until she arrived in England for the wedding. He detested her on sight. She was coarse and clumsy; she also proved to be mentally unstable. It was, from the first, a disastrous alliance. On 7th January, 1796, Caroline gave birth to their daughter, Princess Charlotte; soon afterwards the Prince demanded an immediate and final separation. When Princess Charlotte was old enough, she was brought up by governesses; and when her mother's conduct became a subject for

Carlton House is very beautiful, and magnificent, and we were well amused looking at it yesterday. I don't know whether you are *worthy* of the beauties of old china vases, gold fringes, damask draperies, and all the other fine things we saw there. I can only tell you the lustre in one of the rooms, of glass and ormolu, looking like a shower of diamonds, cost between *two and three thousand pounds*. I write the number at full length, that you mayn't fancy I have put a cypher too many. However, it is such a peculiarly English manufactory that our heir-apparent is right in encouraging it.

The Prince was not content with alterations to Carlton House. Since he now admired the architecture of Humphry Repton, he thought of improving the Pavilion at Brighton, in Indian style. Economy prevented him from doing so. But the interior of the Pavilion was none the less exotic; and Lady Bessborough "did not think the strange Chinese shapes and columns could have looked so well. It is," she wrote, "like Concetti in Poetry, in Outré and false taste, but for the kind of thing as perfect as it can be." Mr Creevey, the diarist, gave a happy account of Brighton domesticity: the Prince instructing his band, the footmen passing sandwiches and wine at the end of the evening, and Mrs Fitzherbert, a keen card-player, absorbed in loo or whist.

In 1807, Mrs Fitzherbert lost her influence over the Prince. He was always susceptible, and he had become infatuated with the middle-aged Lady Hertford. It was a tragic separation. Mrs Fitzherbert deserved every word of praise that she was given. She had never abused her unparalleled power, never lost her dignity. The tragedy of the Prince's life was the fact that "Mrs Fitz." was not born a Protestant Princess. Even his official wife, the Princess of Wales, declared that Mrs Fitzherbert was his true wife. She remained loyal to him all her life; and, despite his infidelities, he remained faithful to her. When he died, twenty-three years later, her portrait was buried with him.

In 1810, the Prince's youngest sister, Princess Amelia, died at the age of twenty-seven. She was said to be the King's favourite child, and the shock of her death overwhelmed him. He now lapsed into permanent insanity. On 31st December, the Prime Minister, Spencer Perceval, moved in the House of Commons that the Regency should be offered to the Prince of Wales, subject to certain restrictions. These restrictions were to last for a year, and for six weeks of the following session of Parliament.

On 6th February, 1811, the Prince of Wales became Prince

Regent. A young society woman, Serena Holroyd, confided to a friend: "It is utterly impossible for me to look forward with any confidence to him. I certainly prefer him to Bonaparte."

The Prince Regent promptly announced that he would continue his father's government in office. While his powers were restricted, he determined to act as the King would have done. That summer, George III was assailed by wilder delusions than ever, and it was clear that in 1812 the Regent would enjoy complete sovereign powers. More than once he suggested a coalition government, but his suggestions were rejected. In June, 1812, he chose a Tory administration, and appointed Lord Liverpool Prime Minister. It was not an irresponsible move, but it alienated him from the Whigs. He became the butt of Whig politicians. He was libelled by the journalist Leigh Hunt. "This Adonis in Loveliness *was a corpulent gentleman of fifty* . . . who has just closed half a century without one single claim on the gratitude of his country or the respect of posterity."

Leigh Hunt was fined, and sentenced to two years' imprisonment. Corpulent though he might be, the Regent had earned, and would still deserve, respect. In the very month when Hunt's libel appeared, *Childe Harold's Pilgrimage* made Byron the lion of London society. The Regent asked to meet him, and Byron was conquered.

> There, too, he saw (whate'er he may be now)
> A Prince, the Prince of Princes at the time,
> With fascination in his very bow,
> And full of promise, as the spring of prime . . .

The Regent talked to Byron on poetry and poets, and showed an understanding and critical taste which at once surprised and delighted him. He said some pleasing things about Byron's work, and Byron dreamed of being Poet Laureate.

For the moment, Byron admired the Regent. Tom Moore had turned against him. A young and ambitious Irishman, Moore had once dedicated a book to him, and found him "beyond doubt a man of very fascinating manners". When the Whigs had failed to get into office, Moore had lost all hope of advancement, and in 1813, with more Irish humour than prudence, he published a little book of political squibs: *Intercepted Letters, or the Twopenny Post-Bag.* Out of his *Post-Bag* tottered a flaccid caricature of a Regent. The book gained Moore notoriety, but it put him beyond the pale.

It sometimes seemed as if the distinguished writers of the age were so blinded by the Regent's disastrous marriage, by some mistaken loyalty to his wife, that they could not recognise his merits. Shelley dismissed him as "that crowned coward and villain". Yet if, in the spring and summer of 1812, he had watched the Regent closely, Shelley would have seen his achievements and his qualities; he would have seen an amateur musician giving a handsome concert at Carlton House; he would have seen a lover of art ratifying the Royal Academy papers, and expressing the hope that his bronze lamp was suitable for the Academy's Great Room. If Shelley had attended the levée on 8th April, he would have seen that science, too, was encouraged. That day the Regent knighted Humphry Davy, the chemist. "The works of scientific men," wrote Davy, "are like the atoms of gold, of sapphire and diamonds, that exist in a mountain . . . When sovereigns are at the expense of digging out these riches, they are repaid by seeing them gems in their crowns." In 1815 Davy invented the safety lamp for miners.

These years were in many ways the most glorious years of the Regency. In December, 1812, Wellington cleared the French from southern Spain, and Napoleon's Grande Armée was in full retreat. In April, 1813, Wellington began his final advance through the Peninsula. In 1813, the Regent's favourite architect, John Nash, started work on the street that would one day be known as Regent Street. In time Nash also altered Carlton House, and designed a series of rooms, including a Gothic Library and a Golden Drawing-Room. Through these royal and splendid rooms, many royal and splendid visitors would pass.

On 3rd June, 1814, the guns in Hyde Park fired salvoes to mark the signing of the Definitive Treaty. The Napoleonic Wars were officially over. On 7th June, an illuminated London received the Allied Sovereigns: Alexander I of All the Russias, and Frederick William III, King of Prussia. While the multitude was applauding, the Regent showed his sense of occasion. He commissioned Thomas Lawrence to paint Alexander and Frederick William, General Blücher, and Count Platoff – whose twenty regiments of Cossacks had devastated the Grande Armée on the retreat from Moscow. Now, for the first time, he expressed his intention of sitting to Lawrence. Henceforward he was Lawrence's best patron.

The Emperor and the King of Prussia visited a respectable number of English institutions: among them the theatre at Covent Garden, the races at Ascot, and Oxford. On 25th June (while Turner

The Prince Regent and the Allied Sovereigns review troops in Hyde Park after the signing of the Definitive Peace Treaty in 1814. The Napoleonic Wars were officially over.

sketched the scene), the Fleet was reviewed at Portsmouth. The Emperor of All the Russias issued a proclamation praising "England, which for twenty years has shaken the colossus of crimes that threatens the universe". Then the princes and potentates departed.

On 1st August came the centenary of the House of Hanover; and the Regent determined to celebrate it in style. Temples, towers, pagodas and drinking booths were set up in Hyde Park, and a mock naval battle was staged on the Serpentine.

> ST VINCENT hide thy fallen head,
> And mourn, alas! thy glories fled;
> But shout his fame, this fleet who plann'd,
> The first best *toyman* in the land! . . .
>
> Thou star of elegance and fashion!
> Thou pink of all that's gay and dashing!
> Graceful *em-bon-point* Adonis!
> Prince of modern macaronies!
>
> Long thou'st been the admiration
> Of a wise and thinking nation!
> Oft thou hast surprised us truly,
> Time past gone as well as newly;

But this *last* grand thought astounds us –
Yes its brilliancy confounds us –
All thy former prodigies,
The world must own, *were fools to this*.

So Peter Pindar wrote in his poem, *The Regent's Fleet*. The Regent
had long been attacked for the vagaries (and the misfortunes) of his
private life; he had been attacked for his lavish expenditure on
entertainment, on building, on works of art, on food and on clothes.
Posterity may admire the man who fostered the art of living; but
few of his contemporaries admired him. In 1814, when he celebrated the centenary of his dynasty, satirists buzzed round, again,
to make their stinging comments on the royal extravagance, and
some were personally offensive to him. It is remarkable that a
sovereign could have been so despised at such a moment of national
ascendancy. No one would withstand the armies which Wellington
commanded, the navy which had proved itself, nine years earlier, at
Trafalgar. No one challenged the immense and widening British
Empire, or doubted its political influence. No one questioned the
wealth of Great Britain, or the capacity of Englishmen to write fine
poems and design noble cities. The spread of popular education, the
interest in social and penal reform, the eagerness to build churches,
and to propagate the Gospel at home and abroad: there was much
about England to respect. But the Prince Regent earned no respect
from the vast mass of his subjects. He was generally hissed in the
streets of London. The overwhelming majority of Englishmen would
never forgive him for his treatment of his wife and daughter.

Everyone must have known the terms on which he had been driven
into dynastic marriage; but none of his subjects, who showed such
vociferous hatred, seems to have considered the prospect of marriage
with an unbalanced and amoral woman.

In the summer of 1814, the Princess of Wales left the country;
for the next six years she travelled abroad, a subject of constant
scandal. The Regent soon had other, graver pre-occupations. On
26th February, 1815, dissatisfied at being Emperor of the Isle of
Elba, Napoleon escaped to France, and the Hundred Days began.
Louis XVIII, who had been restored to his throne by the Allies, fled
from his capital. All last year's celebrations of peace had been premature. On the news of Napoleon's landing in France, the Regent
declared his intention of joining the Allies. England, Austria, Russia
and Prussia bound themselves by treaty not to lay down their arms

An elegant decoration made for the peace celebrations of 1814: Ackermann's transparency. The Angel of Peace may be seen above; below are
the figures of Faith, Hope and Charity, flanked by those of Britannia and
Justice.

until Napoleon was finally vanquished. On 5th April, Wellington took command of the Allied forces in Belgium.

On 18th June, the Hundred Days ended with Waterloo. On the evening of the 21st, an English Member of Parliament, sitting in Brooks's Club, in London, heard shouting in the street. He looked

These celebrations of peace proved, however, to be premature. Napoleon escaped from Elba, and returned to France. He was finally defeated at Waterloo (18 June, 1815), and fled from the field of battle (top). On 15 July he surrendered aboard HMS *Bellerophon* (above).

out to see one of Wellington's staff clattering past in a chaise. He had come from the battlefield to announce the victory to the Regent, and he brought the Napoleonic standards and eagles, the insignia of the Grande Armée. He found the Regent at a party in St James's Square, and he laid the insignia at his feet. The Regent knighted him immediately. On 8th July, Louis XVIII re-entered Paris. On 15th July, Napoleon surrendered to the captain of H.M.S. *Bellerophon*. On 8th August, after asking the Regent in vain for asylum in England, he sailed on the *Northumberland* to St Helena.

During the Hundred Days, the Regent had knighted Thomas Lawrence. Now that the Battle of Waterloo was becoming an old story, the Louvre had to be stripped of its treasures: the works of art which Napoleon had taken from all over Europe had to be restored to their rightful owners. The expense of returning statues to Rome was so heavy that the Pope offered all the sculpture to the Regent. The Regent refused to take advantage of the Pope's financial straits, and paid for the statues to be returned to Italy.

In the winter after Waterloo he found another way to endear himself to posterity. He learned that Jane Austen was in London. He much admired her novels, often read them, and kept a set, as she was told, "in every one of his residences". His librarian was commanded to invite Miss Austen to Carlton House, to pay her every attention, and to say that she was free to dedicate a novel to His Royal Highness. *Emma* was duly dedicated to him.

In 1814, in the suite of the Emperor of Russia, Prince Leopold of Coburg had come to London. Handsome, romantic and politically insignificant, he seemed an ideal husband for the Regent's daughter. Early in 1815, when she had rejected the Prince of Orange, and had been disappointed in her love for Prince Frederick of Prussia, Princess Charlotte had recognised Leopold as a means of gaining independence. She had fallen in love, not so much with Leopold, as with the thought of Leopold the liberator. In January, 1816, the Prince received an invitation to England; he also received a note from the Foreign Secretary, telling him that the Regent intended to give him Princess Charlotte's hand. In February he arrived in Brighton. He was cold and ambitious, and Princess Charlotte was cool and practical; but, long before they married on 2nd May, it was clear that, for Princess Charlotte, a marriage of convenience had become a marriage of love.

Princess Charlotte of Wales and Prince Leopold of Coburg after their marriage in 1816. The Princess was the Regent's only child by his marriage to Caroline of Brunswick.

The next few months were, in many ways, among the happiest in the Regent's life. The Napoleonic Wars were over, his wife was safely abroad, and his daughter was happily married. The government allowed him to satisfy his love of splendour, and he was busy altering his palaces. The year brought many proofs of his interest in the arts and sciences. He acquired a new Rembrandt, and recommended the House of Commons to value the Elgin Marbles, newly arrived from Greece (in June he was granted a sum for the purchase). He knighted William Herschel, the venerable astronomer who had discovered the planet Uranus; and he established himself as a gourmet, by acquiring the services of the legendary *chef de cuisine*, Antonin Carême. Carême had learned his art in Napoleon's kitchens; a few days after he came to Carlton House, he made his impressive English *début*: he contrived twenty *entrées* for a banquet which the Regent was giving for the Grand Duke Nicholas of Russia.

25

George III had gloried in the name of Briton. No English monarch gloried in it more than his eldest son. In 1811, he had assured the Royal Academy that "He felt proud as an Englishman that He might with confidence expect that as this country had risen superior to all others in Arms, in military & naval prowess, so would it in Arts." Now, in 1817, the celebration of the Regent's birth was altered from 12th August, his birthday, to 23rd April, St George's Day. And on 18th June, 1817, the second anniversary of the Battle of Waterloo, he delightedly opened what had been begun as the Strand Bridge, but was now called Waterloo Bridge. Lady Stanley of Alderley, who watched the ceremony, declared that "all and everything conspired in the air above, the earth below, and the waters which flowed under Waterloo Bridge, to make it the most glorious, beautiful, and gratifying spectacle that ever was exhibited".

On 6th November, the Regent's happiness was destroyed. Princess Charlotte died, after giving birth to a stillborn son. She had been the only issue, the only justification, of his wretched marriage to Caroline; she alone had ensured him that his crown would descend to his own line of kings. In his erratic fashion, he had loved her. "The loss of the Dear Princess Charlotte to us is irreparable!" wrote Benjamin Robert Haydon, the historical painter. "She was our rallying point, our hope, our sunny land of promise & consolation. She was young and would have brought to the Throne all the better feelings of experience & youth . . ." The problem of the succession now became urgent, complex and bitter. The Regent was gathering evidence of his wife's wild conduct abroad, and more than once there was talk of a divorce. But, alas, the project came to nothing. His brothers, the Royal Dukes, determined to do their dynastic duty. On 13th July, 1818, in Queen Charlotte's drawing-room at Kew Palace, the Duke of Clarence (the future William IV) married Princess Adelaide of Saxe-Meiningen. The Duke of Kent became the husband of the Princess of Leiningen, the widowed sister of Prince Leopold. They were to be the parents of Queen Victoria.

A few months later, on 17th November, Queen Charlotte died, in her seventy-fifth year. The King lived on at Windsor, no longer an inhabitant of this world. He often talked of his own death, and he used to say: "I must have a new suit of clothes, and I will have them black, in memory of George III."

On 29th January, 1820, he died at last. The Regency was over, and the reign of George IV began.

II. THE SOCIAL SCENE

IT IS DIFFICULT to conjure up a mental picture of Regency England. It lies one hundred and sixty years away; an industrial revolution and two world wars separate it from us. In 1811, when the
Regency began, England was the centre of a vast and expanding
empire, but it was still largely an agricultural nation. The English
countryside remained much as Constable painted it. Towns and
cities remained as they should be, an organic part of the scene: they
had grown and matured over centuries, they were free of tasteless
jerry-building. Suburbia was mercifully unknown. The lord lived
in his castle, the squire in his manor, the workman in his unpretentious
cottage. Social classes were clearly defined; and, though there was
social injustice, there was also much contentment for the un-
ambitious. In 1811, when the Regency began, England was still
fighting the long war against Napoleon; but England had not been
invaded, or seriously disturbed. Transport was slow, and com-
munications were far from efficient. The only mass medium was the
Press. It was easy to remain unaware of the outside world. With the
Victorian era, the modern age begins. The Regency lies on the far
side of the chasm.

Like all history, we see it best through the eyes of contemporary
witnesses; and some of the liveliest impressions of Regency England
were left by Richard Rush, the American Minister to the Court of

St James's. Late in December, 1817, he arrived to take up his residence. On 20th December, he set out from Portsmouth for London, and, as his post-chaise bowled along, he looked around him with observant eyes.

At noon, I set out for London. We were soon out of Portsmouth, and went as far as Godalming that day, a distance of 38 miles, over roads like a floor.

I was surprised at the few houses along or near the road side. I had been full of the idea of the populousness of England . . . We rarely met wagons, carriages, or vehicles of any sort, except stage coaches. We did not see a single person on horseback. The stage coaches illustrated what is said of the excellence of that mode of travelling in England. These, as they came swiftly down the hills, or were met in full trot upon the plains, the horses fine, the harness bright, and the inside and out filled with passengers, not only men but women, all well dressed, crowding the tops, had a bold and picturesque appearance. The few peasants whom we saw, were fully and warmly clad. They wore breeches and stockings, a heavy shoe, which, lacing over the ankle, made the foot look clumsy; a linen frock over the coat, worked with plaits, and stout leather gloves, which they kept on while working.

Next day, when Rush continued his journey, he found a marked change in the countryside.

Everything now began to wear a different aspect; the change was more decided after passing Guildford . . . We saw evidence of a more abundant population, and an advanced state of husbandry. The season did not show the country in its best dress; but we were enabled to see more of it by the very absence of the foliage. Farms and common dwellings, with fields beautifully divided and enclosed; country seats, with lodges and stately

The chief means of transport and communication in Regency England: the stage-coach and the mail-coach.

gates of iron marking the entrance to them; lawns fresh and verdant, though it was the winter solstice; parks and pleasure grounds munificently enclosed; ancient trees in avenues, standing in copses, or shooting up among the hedges, with shrubbery tastefully arranged in gardens, and vines and flowers clustering about the houses, were among the objects that rose in succession as we passed along . . . As we got nearer to London, indications multiplied of what had been effected by time and art and wealth to fill up its vast environs . . . All within our view grew more and more instinct with life; until at length, evening coming on, at first villages, then rows of buildings, and people, and twinkling lights, and all kinds of sound, gave token that the metropolis was close by. We entered it by Hyde Park Corner, passing through Piccadilly and Bond Street, beholding the moving crowds which now the town lights revealed.

London was spreading, but it was still clearly separated from the surrounding country. There were no green belt and no suburbia; there were no dreary miles of ribbon development, no rows of factories, no three-line motorways or overpasses to create an ugly no-man's land. There were simply more buildings as one approached the capital. London was already large, but it was a handsome city; and day and night it was astir with purpose and with life. We may recall it in countless engravings and paintings of the time; but, for a sight of Regency London, we must also turn to that devoted Londoner, Charles Lamb. When Wordsworth asked him to Cumberland, he answered in all honesty:

Separate from the pleasure of your company, I don't much care if I never see a mountain in my life. I have passed all my days in London, until I have formed as many and intense local attachments, as any of you mountaineers can have done with dead nature. The lighted shops of the Strand and Fleet Street, the innumerable trades, tradesmen and customers, coaches, waggons, playhouses, all the bustle and wickedness about

Covent Garden, the very women of the Town, the Watchmen, drunken scenes, rattles, – life awake, if you awake, at all hours of the night, the impossiblity of being dull in Fleet Street, the crowds, the very dirt & mud, the Sun shining upon houses and pavements, the print shops, the old book stalls, parsons cheapening books, coffee houses, steams of soups from kitchens, the pantomime, London itself a pantomime and a masquerade, – all these things work themselves into my mind and feea me, without a power of satiating me. The wonder of these sights impells me into night-walks about her crowded streets, and I often shed tears in the motley Strand from fulness of joy at so much Life.

Regency London delighted Antonio Canova, the Italian sculptor: "A surprising capital: most beautiful streets, squares and bridges.

Soho Square

Great cleanliness. And what surprises me most is that everywhere I observe the prosperity of mankind." And again, Richard Rush, the American visitor: "I am aware how much larger London is, than Paris; but the bustle of business seemed to abound in the English metropolis in a proportion tenfold greater than its superior size." Rush took a house in Baker Street. It was then far from the bustle; and "on the broad pavements of flag you perhaps saw nobody before noon, unless a straggling servant in morning livery, or a butcher's boy with tray in hand issuing here and there from an area . . ."

Other familiar London figures made their appearance in *City*

The man from whom the Regency takes its name and spirit. When this picture was painted by Lawrence, the Prince Regent had become King George IV.

Scenes; or a Peep into London for Children, which was published in the Regency years. In this simple little book we see the watchman, with "a comfortable great coat, a lantern, and a rattle, with a large stick, to attack thieves". Near him is one of the link boys who were "always at dark crossings and lanes, to light passengers through them". The author of *City Scenes* considered that "they deserve the reward of a few halfpence from those whom they assist". The link boys could still earn some sort of living: only in 1807 had street gas-lights been introduced in Golden Lane; only in 1809 had gas been used in lighting streets and houses in Pall Mall. But London and, indeed, the whole country, grew steadily brighter: by 1821, the year after the Regency ended, gaslight had been introduced into nearly every town in Great Britain. In Regency days, when the link boys were still busy, the nosegay-seller and flower-pot man still enlivened the London streets; the watercress girl and the dairymaid with her cow reminded Londoners that the country was not far distant. And –

A PEEP at the GAS LIGHTS in PALL-MALL.

for the eighteenth century was only a dozen years or so away – one might still see occasional chairmen carrying a traveller in a sedan chair; but these chairs, said the guide, were seldom used, "except for the sick and weakly, and courtiers attending the Prince Regent's levées".

And here, perhaps, we might ourselves visit Carlton House. We might wander across the lawns, where the peacocks are strutting, admire the Rose Satin Drawing-room, the Blue Velvet Room, the Golden Drawing-room, the Gothic Dining-room, and the Gothic Conservatory. We might well choose to appear on 19th June, 1811, when the Prince Regent gives a grand entertainment.

More than two hundred guests had supper in his garden, sheltered by awnings, and surrounded by "festoons of flowers, yielding the most odoriferous perfumes, and relieved by the verdant and softer beauties that more towering plants and shrubs could bestow". The official account of this evening recalls the romantic charm, the fantastic splendour, the inspired originality, which the Regent brought to the art of living.

The arched roofs were ornamented in the liveliest manner, and from them were suspended thousands of lights, in all the different forms and fashions by which illumination can be produced. The *coup-d'œil* of the whole . . . was inexpressibly delightful, and even magically impressive . . . The long range of supper-rooms on the garden level, at the head of which the Regent sat, at the west end of the conservatory, inspired the highest ideas of regal magnificence . . . The appearance of the conservatory was truly striking and brilliant. The architecture of it is of the most delicate Gothic. The upper end was a kind of circular buffet, surmounted by a medallion, with the initials G.P.R. The conservatory was lined by festoons and antique draperies of pink and silver, and partly filled by mirrors, before which, on ornamented shelves, stood a variety of vases, candlesticks, &c. of the most gorgeous gold plate . . .

The male part of the nobility and gentry were habited in court suits, many richly embroidered, or in military or naval uniforms. The waving plumage – the elegant variegated dresses – the sparkling diamonds – and, still more, the native beauty and grace of the ladies gave a sort of enchanting perfection to the whole of this brilliant courtly exhibition . . .

The upper servants of His Royal Highness's household wore a rich costume of dark blue, trimmed with very broad gold lace: the others wore their state liveries. A considerable number of the yeomen of the guard attended in different parts . . . Two of the bands of the Guards, in state uniform, played various airs throughout the night.

Some of the pleasures of the Regency: boxing, grouse-shooting, and hunting. The Prince Regent was a great patron of the ring and is said to have driven the boxer Tom Spring through the streets of London. The caricature of the stag hunt is by Thomas Rowlandson.

The leading actor was worthy of his setting. The *Morning Chronicle* reported:

His Royal Highness the Prince Regent entered the State Apartments about a quarter past nine o'clock, dressed in a scarlet coat, most richly and elegantly ornamented in a very novel style with gold lace, with a brilliant star of the Order of the Garter . . . The conservatory presented the fine effect of a lofty aisle in an ancient cathedral . . . The grand table extended the whole length of the conservatory, and across Carlton House to the length of 200 feet . . . Along the centre of the table, about six inches above the surface, a canal of pure water continued flowing from a silver fountain, beautifully constructed at the head of the table. Its faintly waving artificial banks were covered with green moss and aquatic flowers, gold and silver fish, gudgeons, etc., were seen to swim and sport through the bubbling current, which produced a pleasing murmur when it fell, and formed a cascade at the outlet. At the head of the table, above the fountain, sat His Royal Highness the Prince Regent, on a throne of crimson velvet, trimmed with gold.

Shelley, who detested the Regent, inquired of a friend: "What think you of the *bubbling brooks* and *mossy banks* at Carlton House – the *allées vertes*, etc.? It is said that this entertainment will cost £120,000. Nor will it be the last bauble which the nation must buy to amuse this overgrown bantling of Regency." After the fête, the apartments were open to the public, by ticket, for three days. On the last day there was a stampede, "and of the number of delicate and helpless females who were present, some were thrown down, and,

35

shocking to relate, literally trod upon by those behind, without the possibility of being extricated". There were said to be some 30,000 people.

A few days later came a ball at Devonshire House, "the ball brilliant, from all the women having on their Carlton House gowns, and many their [Court] feathers". Social life was dazzling and in-

A confectioner's shop

tense; the Regent attended assemblies at Lady Hertford's and Lady Stafford's, he again attended the Royal Academy dinner. In the memoirs and letters of the time, we follow him through his Regency: dining with exiled Bourbon princes, watching amateur theatricals, and attending a concert of Ancient Music. Captain Gronow recorded in his *Reminiscences*:

Carlton House was a centre for all the great politicians and wits who were the favourites of the Regent . . . In the rear of the mansion was an extensive garden that reached from Warwick Street to Marlborough House; green sward, stately trees (probably two hundred years old), and beds of the choicest flowers, gave to the grounds a picturesque attraction perhaps unequalled. It was here that the heir to the throne of England gave, in 1813, an open-air *fête*, in honour of the battle of Vittoria. About 3 o'clock p.m., the *élite* of London society . . . began to arrive – all in full dress; the ladies particularly displaying their diamonds and pearls, as if they were going to a drawing-room . . .

The *élite* enjoyed such occasions as much as the Regent himself. That same year Lady Elizabeth Feilding described another royal fête to her sister.

I am afraid all my powers of description would fail to give you an idea of the oriental air of everything in that Mahomet's Paradise, Carlton House. I do not know whether *we* all looked like *Houris*, but I for one was certainly in the 77th heaven . . .

Imagine yourself ascending a flight of steps into an immense saloon lighted up to the ceiling with a profusion of candles and a display of gold plate on either hand that dazzled the eye while a *sonorous* band of turbaned slaves played "God Save the King".

The sight and sound were both animating, the kettle-drums and cymbals, the glitter of spangles and finery, of dress and furniture that burst upon you was quite *éblouissant*.

Then you turned to the right through a suite of rooms, some hung with scarlet and gold, others with blue and gold, and some decorated with portraits of all our great commanders. At last you arrived at the ballroom, where sat the Queen at the upper end, with the Princesse de Condé on her right hand, and the Russian Ambassadress (Comtesse de Lieven) on her left. This last was a most singular figure; she was in black velvet up to her chin, with a huge ruff like Queen Elizabeth, or rather more like Mary Queen of Scots, for she is very handsome. She had no ornaments whatever but a long chain of *very* large diamonds, and a picture that hung *on her back*. Her head was dressed quite flat, and she looked exactly like something walked out of its frame in an old picture gallery . . .

In June 1814, came the visit of the Allied Sovereigns. There were countless banquets and entertainments, and one evening the royal visitors dined with the Corporation of London. In front of the royal table

were placed upon the floors, and upon stages, a profusion of the most rare and costly aromatic shrubs . . . The Dinner was as sumptuous as expense or skill could make it, and was served entirely on plate . . . Samuel Turner, Esq., one of the Directors of the Bank of England, very handsomely presented a fine Turtle for the occasion, which was the first imported in the season, and arrived in time to be served . . . A large Baron of Beef, with the Royal Standard, was placed upon a stage at the upper end of the Hall, in view of the Royal Table, attended by the Serjeant Carvers and one of the principal Cooks, in proper costume.

Fifteen toasts were drunk, each of them preceded by a flourish of trumpets. The visit of the Allied Sovereigns was followed by the celebration of the centenary of the House of Hanover. On 21st July the Regent gave a ball at Carlton House for the Duke of Wellington. Lady Harriot Frampton recorded:

The supper laid out in one room for the Queen was very handsome, as the ornaments were quite beautiful. There were fifty covers, and the plateau down the middle of the table was covered with exquisite groups in silver gilt. The centre group was above three feet high, and each one of the figures was so beautifully executed that they might have been ornaments in a drawing-room, and everything else, even the salt-cellars, was in the most excellent taste. All was in gold or silver-gilt, which made the silver plate, set out in the deep-recessed windows, look cold and poor, although in reality it was very massive and handsome.

The plates only were of china and I recognised them as a set of the finest Sèvres porcelain which Lady Auckland had once shown me at Beckenham, as having been a present from Louis XVI to the late Lord Auckland, when he was Ambassador at Paris, and I regretted that they should have been obliged to part with them. Each plate had a large bird painted in the centre of it.

All the rooms were studded with Ws in honour of the Duke of Wellington, who, however, seemed to do all he could to avoid notice.

During this summer, the Prince Regent met the Duke again, at a banquet given by Wellington's brother.

The royal table – laid for thirty people – was raised on a platform at the end of the room. Above it stood a Buffet, laden with gold plate, and surmounted by a bust of the Prince Regent. At the other end of the room stood a table laden with silver plate, surmounted by a bust of the Duke of Wellington . . . The Prince proposed the health of the Duke of Wellington, in a very neat speech. When the Duke rose to reply, the Prince Regent promptly interposed: "My dear fellow, we know your *actions*, and we will excuse your *words*, so sit down."

This the Duke did, with all the delight of a schoolboy who has been given an unexpected holiday!

Outside London, the Regent's life remained elegant and lively. In 1811, Thomas Creevey the diarist found him in Brighton.

Nov. 1st. We were at the Pavilion last night – Mrs Creevey's three daughters, and myself – and had a very pleasant evening . . . About half-past nine, which might be a quarter of an hour after we arrived, the Prince came out of the dining-room. He was in his best humour, bowed and spoke to all of us, and looked uncommonly well, tho' very fat. He

The music-room at the Royal Pavilion, Brighton. Concerts were frequently given there, and the Regent himself often gave directions to his band.

was in his full Field Marshal's uniform. He remained quite as cheerful and full of fun to the last – half-past twelve – asked after Mrs Creevey's health, and nodded and spoke when he passed us . . . The officers of the Prince's regiment had all dined with him, and looked very ornamental monkeys in their red breeches with gold fringe and yellow boots. The Prince's band played as usual in the dining-room till 12, when the pages and footmen brought about iced champagne punch, lemonade and sandwiches . . .

The Prince looked much happier and more unembarrassed by care than I have seen him since this time six years . . . Now that he has the weight of the Empire upon him, he is quite alive . . .

Nov. 2nd. We were again at the Pavilion last night . . . The Regent sat in the Musick Room almost all the time between Viotti, the famous violin player, and Lady Jane Houston, and he went on for hours beating his thighs the proper time for the band, and singing out aloud, and looking about him for accompaniment from Viotti and Lady Jane. It was a curious sight to see a Regent thus employed, but he seemed in high good humour . . .

Left: the night watchman and the linkboy, two sources of light in the
dark streets of London

Above: other people who might be seen in a city street – fireman, barrow
woman, milk girl and lamp-lighter

Maria Fitzherbert. "If ever the Prince loved a woman it was she." They were secretly married in 1785, but the marriage was invalid under the Royal Marriages Act. Her picture was buried with him forty-five years later.

Caroline of Brunswick, the Prince's official wife. He had never seen her before she arrived in England for their wedding in 1795. He detested her on sight.

And so the Regency continued, in a whirl of concerts and banquets, celebrations, assemblies and fancy-dress balls. At Holland House, in Kensington, the redoubtable Lady Holland and her husband attracted Whig politicians, men of letters, dandies, wits and reformers: among them were Samuel Rogers, the poet, Tom Moore (the author of *Intercepted Letters*), and the Reverend Sydney Smith. In 1813, Robert Southey wrote to his wife: "I dined on Sunday at Holland House, with an ill-assorted party of 18 or 20 persons . . . In the evening Lord Byron came in . . ., and I saw a man whom in voice, manner and countenance I liked very much more than either his character or his writings had given me reason to expect."

Some of the most entertaining pictures of aristocratic life were drawn by Maria Edgeworth, the Irish novelist. In the spring and summer of 1813 she found herself in England. She left domestic cares behind her, and happily burst into the wider world, which she described in letters to her family. She dined at Lady Spencer's: "The dinner *au reste* was stupid tho' very grand – 24 candles on the table in superb branches – sideboard of gold plate at one end and silver at the other end." Miss Edgeworth also dined with Thomas Hope, the author of *Household Furniture*, and his wife.

We have been to a grand night at Mrs Hope's – furniture Hope – rooms really deserve the French epithet *superbe*! All of beauty, rank and fashion that London can assemble I believe I may say in the newspaper style was there . . . The Prince Regent stood holding converse with Lady Elizabeth Monck one third of the night – she leaning gracefully on a bronze table in the center of the room . . . About 500 people were at this assembly – The crowd of carriages so great that after sitting an hour waiting in ours, the coachman told us there was no chance of our getting *in* unless we got *out* and walked.

In 1818, Miss Edgeworth paid another visit to England. She stayed at Bowood, and revelled in life in a great country house.

Breakfast at ½ after nine – Breakfast very pleasant tho a servant waits – but he is an Italian a Milanese – seems like a machine who understands only what relates to *his service* – stands by a round table placed in front of a stand of flowers – on this table large silver lamp tea urn – Coffee urn and all necessary for tea and coffee to be made by him. On the large round table at which we sit there appears what looks like an elegant goûter – mixed cut glass and beautiful china – meat–sweetmeats – cakes – buns – rolls &c. in each dish or china basket – numbers of cut glass ewers and cut glass sugar basons. Milanese watches all who enter – *salvers* them with

When Elizabeth Fry visited Newgate Prison in 1813, she found some 300 women in privation and misery. She set out to alleviate their condition. In 1817 she received permission to establish a school and a factory in the prison, and organised an association for prison reform. Her improvements were carried into most of the gaols, asylums and hospitals of Britain.

tea and coffee – and the cups are changed and all continually supplied without hands crossing or any *I'll trouble yous*. I am a convert which I thought I should never be to this system. Conversation goes on delightfully and one forgets the existence of the *dumb waiter*.

October found Miss Edgeworth in a very different setting: staying with Joanna Baillie, the authoress, in the little village of Hampstead, near London.

For 6 or 7 miles as we approached Hampstead the whole country seemed to be what you might call a *citizens paradise* – not a *fools* paradise though a fastidious man of taste or an intolerant philosopher might think them synonymous terms. No here are means of *comfort* and enjoyment more substantial than ever were provided in any fools paradise. Then such *odd* prettinesses – Such a variety of little *snuggeries* and such green trellises and bowers and vinecovered fronts of houses that look as if they had been built and painted in exact imitation of the cottages in the front and side-scenes of Drury-lane . . .

Joanna Baillie and her sister the most kind cordial warm hearted

The Rev. Sydney Smith. His articles in *The Edinburgh Review* expressed the social conscience of the age.

creatures came running down their little flagged walk to welcome us . . .

Wednesday morning. Breakfast time in this house is very pleasant. These two good sisters look so neat and chearful when we meet them in the morning – delicately white tablecloth – *Scotch marmalade* – Excellent tea and coffee – Everything at breakfast and at dinner at all times so neat and suitable! . . . They told us the history of Mrs Fry the quaker who goes to reform the people at Newgate. They know her intimately. She is very rich – very handsome a delicate madona-looking woman – married to a man who adores her and what is much more to the purpose supplies her with money and lets her follow her benevolent *courses* (I did not say *whims*) as she pleases.

Maria Edgeworth describes the routine of middle-class life in the days of the Regency. It is reflected, too, in the diary of Crabb Robinson, the letters of Keats and Lamb and Sydney Smith. But Sydney Smith, the reformer, was more aware than most of the shadow side of the age. In one of his most poignant and indignant articles, he turned from the elegant dinner table to the small boy sent up the chimney to put out the fire. In 1817, in a letter to his publisher, John Murray, Robert Southey discussed his own article on "The Rise and Progress of Popular Disaffection" and his projected book on the state of society. Some social evils could, he wrote, be righted by governments.

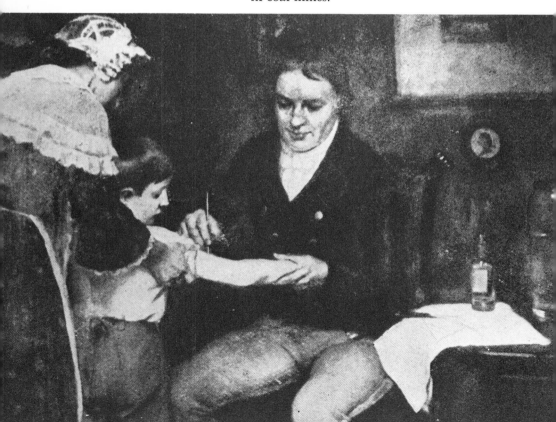

Among these I include the gross ignorance of the people, the ruinous expense and heart-breaking delays of law – the state of our prisons, and those modes of taxation which directly tend to produce violations of the laws, etc., etc. Some hints rather than plans for alleviating some of these evils I shall throw out – such as Protestant nunneries, in which women may find a respectable and comfortable retreat, without vows; asylums for every child who needs one . . . This is certain that no relief is to be expected from employing the poor in manufactures; you only shift the burden, and carry more goods to a market already overstocked; but set them to agriculture, and every man can at least provide for himself and family, if he raises no surplus produce. Things cannot continue as they are.

Edward Jenner and Humphry Davy were recognised by the Regent for their contribution to the general welfare. The picture shows Jenner performing the first vaccination in 1796. Davy invented the Davy lamp (above), known as the safety lamp, after his investigation of explosions in coal mines.

In 1818, Southey published an article in the *Quarterly* "On the Means of Improving the People".

It relates [he told a friend] to the means of improving the lower class, calling for vigilance in the magistrates and parish officers with respect to ale houses; and speaking a good word in recommendation of the stocks. Upon the subject of education there is no choice in this stage of society: it is a ground which if you do not occupy the enemy will: if you do not sow wheat, he will sow tares . . . You can no longer have uncontested, unoffending and submissive ignorance – let us therefore take the people in childhood and teach them what to believe.

In 1801, the first census of Great Britain had shown a population of 10,942,646. In 1811, the year in which the Regency began, the second census recorded a population of 12,552,144. The population steadily increased, but social consciousness developed slowly. Charles Lamb was to write an essay on "The Praise of Chimney-Sweepers":

When a child, what a mysterious pleasure it was to witness their operation! to see a chit no bigger than one's-self enter, one knew not by what process, into what seemed the *fauces Averni* – to pursue him in imagination, as he went sounding on through so many dark stifling caverns, horrid shades! – to revive at hearing his feeble shout of discovered day-light, and then (O fulness of delight), running out of doors, to come just in time to see the sable phenomenon emerge in safety, the brandished weapon of his art victorious like some flag waved over a conquered citadel! I seem to remember having been told, that a bad sweep was once left in a stack with his brush, to indicate which way the wind blew.

Charles Lamb was humane, and a lover of children. Yet, for all his humanity, he did not appear to see the horror of such dangerous child labour; and children still crawled through the mines, dragging trucks of coal to fill the hearths of the prosperous and indifferent.

The great war against Napoleon coincided with the Industrial Revolution. A series of mechanical inventions suddenly turned England into the workshop of the world. Manufacture was revolutionised; and, at the same time, agriculture was transformed by new methods of cultivation and stock-breeding. England could now not only feed her rapidly growing population, but export her produce to the Continent, which had been desolated by the war. While industry and agriculture were revolutionised, the means of communication was enormously developed. When George III ascended the throne in 1760, England had the most primitive transport in

The Regency was an age of social elegance – whether the occasion was a banquet or a picnic. Opposite page: a scene in the banqueting room in the Royal Pavilion, Brighton. This page: a picnic on Prospect Hill, overlooking Longleat.

Rustic figures, drawn by W. H. Pyne. The man on horseback is a pedlar, who sold not only essentials but trinkets, and toys for the children.

Western Europe. In 1837, on the accession of Queen Victoria, the country had 4,000 miles of navigable waterway; the trunk roads were improved out of all recognition; steam navigation had begun, and two lines of rail had been laid down. The economic, social and political results of these changes were enormous. Among them were the stupendous increase of wealth, the rapid growth of population, the rise of new industries and the growth of cities; the development of means of communication; and the expansion of foreign trade.

But, in the year of Waterloo, such benefits lay in the future. In 1815, England was faced with a slump in trade, a gigantic debt, and a discontented populace. Great wars are always followed by an economic slump, but the slump of 1815 was particularly severe and prolonged. When the war was over, and normal conditions were restored, the continental demand for English goods suddenly slackened; prices fell sharply, production was paralysed, and thousands of people found themselves unemployed. In 1816 a meeting was held in London for the relief of starving weavers; but agricultural workers who demanded better conditions were ruthlessly repressed. In 1819, at Manchester, a well-known agitator was due to speak, and the magistrates decided to arrest him before he had spoken. With arrogant stupidity, they sent in a body of yeomen cavalry to control the crowds. The soldiers took violent action against a defenceless gathering of some 80,000 men, women and children in a square near St Peter's Church. Several people were killed, and three or four hundred were injured in what was known as the Massacre of Peterloo.

But the picture was not entirely black. As social unrest became evident, there was a growing need for popular education. The aristocracy and the middle classes could enjoy the benefits of public and grammar schools, and the privileges of Oxford and Cambridge. Now the working classes, too, were beginning to have more than rudimentary education. Towards the end of the Regency, the American Minister, Mr Rush, reported home to the Secretary of State on the last session of Parliament.

Education. I notice the report to the House of Commons, by which it appeared how this great work is advancing in England; for that, whilst in 1812, the number of schools, under the national school system, was only 52, and the pupils 8000, this report shows that the former had risen, in 1818, to above 1400, and the number of pupils to 200,000.

The Conservatory, Carlton House

III. HOUSES AND GARDENS

THE REGENCY was one of the happiest ages for English architecture. The average Regency house was not, perhaps, as solidly built as the Georgian house which preceded it, or the Victorian house which followed it; but it had an elegance which largely matched contemporary furniture and fashion. It had charm, conviction, and a style which still owed more to architects than to builders, more to individual taste than to mass production. It is a style best seen, perhaps, in domestic architecture: in unpretentious small houses, in the residential squares of Brighton and Cheltenham, in the grand perspectives of John Nash's terraces in London. Regency architecture may be seen in some of the most felicitous town-planning in England, and it inspired some delightful detail: delicate balconies and verandas, cupolas and classical mouldings, bow fronts and hooded windows and generous doorways, vistas of white or cream-coloured stucco. Regency architecture has the simplicity dear to English taste; it has (as the period deserves) a touch of theatre. It has an assurance which no later English architecture has equalled.

Many distinguished architects from an earlier age overlapped the years of the Regency. Among them were James Wyatt (1746–1813), the architect of country houses and designer of the Pantheon in London; and George Dance the younger (1741–1825), the namesake and fifth son of the architect of the Mansion House. Dance has one claim to be included among the Regency architects: through his work, and his personal friendship, he encouraged John Soane to set out on his career. Charles R. Cockerell – generally known as Professor Cockerell – was born in 1788. The son of another architect, S. P. Cockerell, he was articled in his father's office, and in 1809 he was personal assistant to Robert Smirke, who was then rebuilding Covent Garden Theatre. In 1810 he left England for a seven years' tour of Greece, Asia Minor and Sicily, and he returned to England to become one of the foremost exponents of classical architecture. However, he received his largest commissions after the death of George IV. So did Sir Robert Smirke (1781–1867), another important figure in the classical tradition. Sir Jeffrey Wyatville, the nephew of Wyatt, was appointed Architect to the King by George IV; he is known for his additions to Windsor Castle – but these were hardly in the Regency style. He earned his knighthood in 1828, when he finished his alterations at Windsor. He also received royal permission to add the suffix "ville" to his family name.

Only half-a-dozen architects are generally associated with Regency architecture. Perhaps the most typical is John Buonarotti Papworth (1775–1847). The son of a stuccoist, he grew up familiar with architects and building. He received his early instruction from the great Palladian, Sir William Chambers; he was later apprenticed to an architect, and then to a builder. He finished his practical education by spending a period with a furniture upholsterer. His architectural practice developed in the London suburbs, and he built houses for bankers and wealthy merchants. He was called to make additions to Holland's Claremont, when Princess Charlotte and Prince Leopold lived there. In 1820 he received the diploma of Architect to the King. From 1824 to 1832 he was doing work at Cheltenham, where he built the Rotunda, laid out the Montpellier estate, designed several terraces and many private houses.

Papworth's *Essay on the Causes of Dry Rot in Buildings*, published in 1803, was the first serious study of the subject. He later produced two volumes of *Architectural Hints*, and, in 1818, he published a work which, so he explained, "seeks to unite with the labours of many eminent men, in an attempt to instill into the public a real love for architecture". It succeeds perfectly in its attempt. *Rural Residences* is a delectable series of designs for villas, cottages, and embellishments for houses and estates. Among the most interesting plans is one for a group of four cottages, designed for labourers, and "adapted

Peacocks on the lawn of Carlton House. George III had given the house to the Prince on his twenty-first birthday, and Henry Holland had turned it into one of the finest palaces in Europe.

to park scenery''. Papworth may explain his plan in a dated style, but he shows both elegance and social awareness:

The habitations of the labouring poor may be rendered ornamental, and the comforts of them increased, at a very trifling charge beyond the cost of common buildings; towards this purpose the annexed plate is designed for four cottages, connected with each other, and under one roof; a mode of building that admits a considerable saving of expense . . .

The porch in which the husbandman rests after the fatigues of the day, ornamented by some flowering creeper, at once affords him shade and repose; neatness and cleanliness . . . bespeak that elasticity of mind, and spring of action, which produce industry and cheerfulness . . .

Papworth was concerned not only with labourers' cottages, but with rural retreats for the gentry, and these he adapted carefully to their settings. Presenting a design for a Gothic cottage, he explained:

55

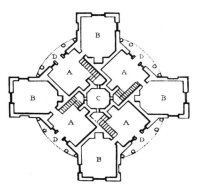

John Papworth's plan for a group of four labourers' cottages, "a mode of building that admits a considerable saving of expense . . ." His cottage *orné* was designed for "the affluent, the man of study, of science, or of leisure".

The cottage *orné* is a new species of building, . . . and subject to its own laws of fitness and propriety. It is not the habitation of the labourers, but of the affluent; of the man of study, of science, or of leisure; it is often the rallying point of domestic comfort, and, in this age of elegant refinement, a mere cottage would be incongruous with the nature of its occupancy. The lawn, the shrubberies, the gravel walks, and the polish that is given to the garden scenery, connected with such habitations, require an edifice in which is to be found a correspondence of tasteful care: perhaps it is essential that this building should be small, and certainly not to exceed two stories; that it should combine properly with the surrounding objects and appear to be native to the spot, and not one of those crude rule-and-square excrescences of the environs of London, the illegitimate family of town and country.

The Gothic cottage was followed by a cottage adapted to romantic scenery, and another one designed (for this was the age of the Lake Poets) "for the neighbourhood of the Lakes". Papworth also created gay and elegant designs for garden seats, and for a veranda which, he considered, was "an useful and ornamental appendage to a London dwelling". In 1823, when the Regency was over, he published *Hints on Ornamental Gardening*, with suggestions for a rustic bridge and a picturesque dairy, this last "designed in imitation of the ruins of a church". In 1835 came his essay on *The Benefits resulting to the manufactures of a Country from a well-directed cultivation of Architecture and of the Art of Ornamental Design*. Papworth himself was a practising designer of "manufactures", especially in metal; among them were a Gothic lantern for Lord Grosvenor, a bronzed chandelier for the Royal College of Surgeons, a chandelier for the Persian Ambassador, and a number of Gothic lustres. In 1818 he designed the interior fittings for the first paddle steamer to ply the Thames. He retired in 1846 and died within a year.

George Basevi (1794–1845) was another typical Regency architect. He was a Londoner, and, since his father's sister married Isaac d'Israeli, he was first cousin to the future Prime Minister. In 1811 he began to study under Sir John Soane, and he is said to have been his favourite pupil. In 1816–19 he made a tour of Italy and Greece, and he returned to become Surveyor to the Guardian Assurance Company. Between 1825 and 1840 he was occupied with building developments in Belgravia and South Kensington. When Nash rebuilt old Buckingham House, and the Court moved from Carlton House to Buckingham Palace, the fields to the west of the new palace were naturally developed. The work was done with imagination and grandeur.

Decimus Burton (1800–1881) lived later into the nineteenth century than any of these architects, but all his major works were done while he was still in his twenties and early thirties. His father, the Bloomsbury builder James Burton, was the contractor for many of Nash's "Metropolitan Improvements". Decimus was brought up as a builder and architect, and began to practise his profession before he was twenty. One of his first buildings was a Regent's Park villa for his father. He designed Cornwall Terrace, Regent's Park, when he was twenty-one, and at twenty-five he built the famous screen and arch at Hyde Park Corner (the arch has since been moved to the top of Constitution Hill). Since he was then an architect to the Office of Woods and Forests, he was also responsible for many of the little lodges and gates which still grace Hyde Park.

Burton began his career as the Regency ended. Henry Holland was born in 1745, and died in 1806, before the Regency was proclaimed, yet he has his association with it. The son of a builder, and the son-in-law of "Capability" Brown, the landscape gardener, his first important commission was to build Claremont House, at Esher, for Lord Clive; it was the house in which Princess Charlotte would spend her married life. This commission brought him patronage, and in 1778 he built Brooks's Club, St James's Street, the meeting-place for the leading Whigs. Through this association, he was introduced to the Prince of Wales (who showed pronounced Whig sympathies in his youth), and he was soon entrusted with the rebuilding of Carlton House. The palace survived its architect by only twenty years. It was, alas, demolished to make way for Waterloo Place and Nash's Carlton House Terraces, and its Ionic colonnade was incorporated in the new National Gallery. In the same year as he started his work on Carlton House, Holland began to redesign the Pavilion at Brighton which had been leased to the Prince of Wales. This was soon to be designed again, and altered out of all recognition, but Holland's cupola may have suggested the Indian domes of Repton and Nash.

Sir John Soane (1753–1837) was exactly Nash's contemporary. As an architect he was more scholarly and individual, but he lacked the dynamism and powers of persuasion which carried Nash into the Regent's favour. Soane was the son of a Reading stonemason, and he began his working life by running errands for George Dance the younger. Dance gave him architectural training and sent him

Two elegant garden seats and an "alcove" designed by Papworth

to Henry Holland, with whom he stayed until 1776. That year he won the Royal Academy Gold Medal, for a design for a triumphal arch. He then went on a travelling scholarship to Italy and Greece. He returned in 1780 and built up a considerable practice; in 1788, in competition, he won the post of architect to the Bank of England. Between 1794 and 1823 he rebuilt the Bank, and it is mainly on this building that his reputation is founded. Though it was classical in spirit, Soane dispensed with many of the features of classicism; his Halls, boldly modelled with Byzantine forms, are preserved in the rebuilt Bank today. His other great public building, the Law Courts at Westminster (1827), was demolished in 1884. His wealthy marriage enabled him to collect works of art and antiquities, and to build the house in Lincoln's Inn Fields which he left to the nation as Sir John Soane's Museum.

The Regency architect *par excellence* is, however, John Nash (1752–1835); indeed he is best known as architect to the Prince Regent. He was born in London, the son of an engineer and millwright, and he began his career in the office of the architect Sir Robert Taylor, where he remained for about ten years. In 1778 he set up as an architect and builder, but in 1783 he went bankrupt, and moved to make

Sir John Soane is chiefly remembered as the architect of the Bank of England (above), but he also left the house in Lincoln's Inn Fields which is known as Sir John Soane's Museum.

Some of Nash's designs for picturesque cottages in Blaise Hamlet, near Bristol

a fresh start in Carmarthen. He became well established as a country-house architect, designing adaptations of the classical, Gothic and picturesque styles. In about 1796 he returned to London, and went into partnership with Humphry Repton, the landscape gardener. It was apparently from the time of his marriage, in 1798, that Nash acquired the patronage of the Prince Regent, and a fortune which allowed him to live in an imposing town house, 29 Dover Street, and to build himself East Cowes Castle, Isle of Wight.

His major work, begun in 1811, was the development of Regent's Park as a residential area, linked by a new street to Carlton House and the centre of London. This development incorporated the Regent's Canal, churches, artisans' houses, shops and arcades, and the layout of many surrounding streets. The Prince, Tom Moore, the poet, reported, "is to have a villa upon Primrose Hill, connected by a fine street with Carlton House, and is so pleased with this magnificent plan, that he has been heard to say, 'it will quite eclipse Napoleon' ''. The villa was not built, but in 1824 Moore "drove . . . to the Regent's Park, with which [he] was enchanted". Crabb Robinson, the diarist, also drove round the Park in a gig, and pronounced his verdict: "I really think this enclosure, with the new street leading to

Nash is probably best remembered for the development of Regent's Park and the area surrounding it. Top, Hanover Lodge. Above, the east side of Park Crescent

it from Carlton House, will give a sort of glory to the Regent's government, which will be more felt by remote posterity than the victories of Trafalgar and Waterloo." The new street was not known as Regent Street until after the Regency was over. It was opened for general thoroughfare in 1821, and it was finished in about 1825, by which time Nash had built the circular church at the northern end: All Souls', Langham Place. Regent Street was, un-

The Music Room at the Royal Pavilion symbolises the genius of the
Regency and its outstanding architect, John Nash.

Cumberland Terrace

The street that connected the new Regent's Park with Carlton House, at the centre of London, became known as Regent Street only after the Regency.

forgivably, demolished in the present century; Nash's nine terraces round Regent's Park have been converted into flats and offices, though we may still admire their façades. Park Crescent was much damaged by bombs during the Second World War, but it has been restored to its former state, and we may still appreciate the charm of Park Village East, and the handsome exterior of Carlton House Terrace.

In October, 1812, the Treasury ordered that a cottage in Windsor Great Park should be remodelled as a temporary home for the Regent. They finally ordered that it should be a permanent residence for the Regent and his household. Nash, as the Woods and Forests architect, was responsible for the alterations. He was anxious to make the cottage look as small as possible. He gave the entrance-front two gables and a Gothic door. The garden front, long and low, had little thatched bonnets on the roof, and a little rustic veranda below, where honeysuckle grew. The conservatory was built of cast-iron trellised pilasters with a trellised temple in the centre. It was

Chester Terrace

painted green, and Nash devised plantations around it. The result was "a dwelling place at once royal and rustic, on the outside the simplicity of a cottage, within the rarest reunion of comfort, elegance and magnificence".

From 1813 to 1815, Nash was Deputy Surveyor-General; he had also become the Prince Regent's personal architect, and as such he extended and greatly altered the Royal Pavilion, Brighton (1815–23), in a fanciful "Hindoo" style, at a total cost of about £160,000. Among his first additions were the Great Kitchen, and the Long Gallery with its staircase. The two new State Apartments, the

The saloon, Royal Pavilion, Brighton

Banqueting and Music Rooms, were added in 1817. In August, 1818, the Regent came down to Brighton with Nash and "several eminent artists" to devise further alterations; he saw the iron framework of the new sixty-ton dome put together during his stay. Between 1818 and 1821 the middle part of the building was transformed. In December, 1818, Mr Croker of the Admiralty went to look at the Pavilion, and left some lively comments upon it.

It is not so much changed as I had been told [so he reported] . . . But in the place of the two rooms which stood at angles of 45° with the rest of the building . . . have been erected two immense rooms, sixty feet by forty;

John Nash, the pre-eminent
architect of the Regency.
From the portrait by
Sir Thomas Lawrence

one for a music-room and the other for a dining-room. They both have
domes; an immense dragon suspends the lustre of one of them. The music-
room is most splendid, but I think the other handsomer. They are both
too handsome for Brighton, and in an excessive degree too fine for the
extent of His Royal Highness's premises. It is a great pity that the whole
of this suite of rooms was not solidly built in or near London. The outside
is said to be taken from the Kremlin at Moscow; it seems to me to be
copied from its own stables, which perhaps were borrowed from the
Kremlin. It is, I think, an absurd waste of money, and will be a ruin in
half a century or sooner.

Happily, Mr Croker's predictions were not to be fulfilled. The Pavilion remains to delight posterity; and even a Victorian critic,
Edward Brayley, was lost in admiration of the music-room.

No verbal description, however elaborate, can convey to the mind or
imagination of the reader an appropriate idea of the magnificence of this
apartment . . .
   The windows, which are so contrived as to be illuminated from the
exterior, are enriched with stained glass displaying numerous Chinese
devices, and similar decorations, in green gold, surround them . . .
   At the apex [of the cupola], expanding in bold relief and vivid colour-

69

ing, is a vast foliated ornament, bearing a general resemblance to a sun-flower, with many smaller flowers issuing from it in all the luxuriancy of seeming cultivation. From this, apparently projected from the calyx, depends a very beautiful lustre of cut glass, designed in the pagoda style, and sustaining by its chain-work an immense lamp in the form of the *nelumbrium*, or water-lily. The upper leaves are of white ground glass, edged with gold, and enriched with transparent devices derived from the mythology of the Chinese; the lower leaves are of a pale crimson hue. At the bottom are golden dragons in attitudes of flight . . .

In 1818, Mr Croker had made his comments on the banqueting room. "After dinner the new dining-room was lighted, and [His Royal Highness] took the ladies to see it. It is really beautiful . . . The ceilings of both the [music-room and the dining-room] are spherical and yet there is no echo. Nash says that he has avoided it by some new theory of sound, which he endeavoured to explain, and which I did not understand, not I believe he either. The rooms are as full of lamps as Hancock's shop." Mr Brayley was more en-thusiastic. "The windows, which are glazed lozenge-wise, include in their embellishments radiant suns within circles, on a blue ground, involving dragons and serpents in their blaze, in accordance with oriental imagery." As for the cupola, "an Eastern sky, partially obscured by the broad and branching foliage of a luxuriant and fruited plantain tree, is depicted on the upper part; and from this appears to issue a vast dragon, finely carved and brilliantly coloured, the wings and scales being redolent of metallic green and silver". From the dragon's claws hangs a chandelier which cost £5613 9s, and weighs nearly a ton.

The only rooms in the Pavilion which earned Mr Croker's cordial approval were the kitchens. "The kitchen and larder are admirable – such contrivances for roasting, boiling, baking, stewing, frying, steaming and heating; hot plates, hot closets, hot air, and hot hearths, with all manner of cocks for hot water and cold water and warm water and steam, and twenty saucepans all ticketed and labelled, placed up to their necks in a vapour bath." Among the final improvements was the addition of the King's Apartments in 1819.

In 1821 instructions were given that Buckingham House should be rebuilt as a royal palace. But George IV – as the Regent had become – died in 1830, and Nash's work at Buckingham Palace was never completed. He shared his master's unpopularity, and he was dis-missed.

Humphry Repton, Nash's
partner, was primarily known
as a landscape gardener.

Humphry Repton had been the partner of Nash, but he was much
more than assistant to that forceful and much-publicised architect.
He was the leading landscape gardener of his time. He was born at
Bury St Edmunds, in Suffolk, in 1752, and as a young man he had a
mercantile business in Norwich. A financial setback soon after his
marriage led him to retire, and in 1788 he decided to exploit his
interest in landscape gardening. It was five years since the death of
"Capability" Brown, and Brown had left no successor. Repton soon
established a wide reputation. In 1794 he published *Sketches and
Hints on Landscape Gardening*. It was the most remarkable analysis of
the English school yet made, and it remained the basis of study even
in the twentieth century. Repton was not content with suggesting
general principles: he designed individual estates and gardens. He
prepared schemes in the form of books, usually bound in red leather.
These contained his written proposals, illustrated by water-colour
sketches, many of which had moveable flaps to show the "before and
after" effects. Repton claimed that he had prepared some 400 of
these Red Books for his clients, but fewer than half of them seem to
have survived.

Some of Repton's designs for the Royal Pavilion at Brighton: above, garden improvements; right, designs for the pheasantry and the vinery

In about 1805, he was summoned to Brighton to suggest improvements for the Pavilion. He arrived full of Indian ideas. "Mr Repton," said the Prince, "I consider the whole of this work as perfect, and will have every part of it carried into immediate execution." The plans were, alas, abandoned on grounds of economy; but in 1808, three years before the Regency began, Repton published his *Designs for the Pavillon at Brighton*. They show delightful imagination, gaiety and splendour. In 1816, in Regency days, he also published his *Fragments on the Theory and Practice of Landscape Gardening*. It was dedicated to the Prince Regent; and no one with an affection for the period, with a taste for its architecture, interior decoration and landscape design, could fail to be entranced by this book. As we study the "before and after" illustrations, we see the inspired landscape gardener at work: planting woods, creating lakes, clearing vistas, hiding ungainly sights, conjuring up a rose-garden or a stately home. It is a fascinating demonstration of the man of taste using his mind and his imagination. Here are the vinery, the forcing-garden in

Repton's sketches of the view from his own cottage in Essex, before (above) and after his improvements

winter, and the view that Repton himself loved best: the view from his own cottage in Essex. And, since he is concerned with the common people as well as the nobility and gentry, he designs a new workhouse in Kent, and delivers a moral homily:

In addition to the usual employment of the Paupers in the Work-rooms, it were to be wished that more wholesome and useful labour might be taught to the Children than spinning, and other manufactures. This might be considered as the reward of good conduct: the Children, supplied with spades, and hoes, and tools, proportioned to their strength, should be taught and exercised in the cultivation of the Garden, and perhaps drilled to become the future defenders of their Country.

This sketch will in some degree explain the effect of this scene as viewed from the high road. We may suppose the warm benches along the front of the building occupied by the aged and infirm, who may there enjoy their few remaining days of sunshine . . . On the warm tiles of the central building some vines may be trained, and the produce of these, and every part of the Garden, such as fruit and flowers, may be exposed to sale on the public road, and the profits of these commodities might be the reward of extraordinary industry or good behaviour.

Repton was influenced by the Picturesque movement, which admired wild landscapes, but his landscapes were seldom as large as Capability Brown's, and they tended to be more thickly planted. He was conscious of the relation of architecture to landscape, and he took a particular interest in cottages, lodges, conservatories, and what he called "winter corridors". He died in 1818.

He had worked at a critical moment in garden design. The Royal Horticultural Society had been founded in 1804, and, after the Battle of Trafalgar the following year, explorers and naturalists were free to roam all over the world. New species of trees, especially conifers, shrubs and flowers, altered the traditional English scene. The landscape movement coincided with England's rise to world power, and English landscape and ideas remained predominant until the early twentieth century. However, by 1840 the original creative force was spent, and the art of landscape planning, as opposed to gardening, did not revive for at least a hundred years.

The interiors of the houses designed by Papworth and Basevi, Burton and Nash, the houses which stood in Repton's romantic landscapes, had an elegance which – a few years hence – was to vanish from most English homes. The Regency – and the reign of George IV, which was virtually its continuation – was one of the finest periods for English domestic architecture, and for the interior decoration of the English house.

Humphry Repton's *Fragments on the Theory and Practice of Landscape Gardening* was dedicated to the Prince Regent; it included designs for a "Forcing Garden, in Winter" and "The Work House". Repton's workhouse is idyllic: children learn the arts of cultivation as well as being "drilled to become the future defenders of their Country". The fruits of the garden "may be exposed to sale on the public road", and it is suggested that "the profits of these commodities might be the reward of extraordinary industry or good behaviour".

76

It was the last epoch before the Industrial Revolution substituted manufacture for craftsmanship, before mass production and the rapid rise of the middle classes coarsened and cheapened design. Cottages and simple country houses in Regency days were furnished with plain and satisfying chairs and tables and beds: the work and pride of individual furniture-makers and craftsmen. They had an honest, natural simplicity, they were as much part of the houses in which they stood as the local stone or brick of which the walls were built. They were free of foreign influence, they were wholly English, they were part of the organic whole. They suggested the unpretentious way of life of the great mass of Englishmen.

Three light bedroom chairs show the elegance which is found in all Regency furniture.

When, in 1818, Papworth designed his cottage "for the neighbourhood of the Lakes", he also left instructions for the interior decoration. They remain a model of Regency taste.

The parlour, the music-room and the lobby are very simply and neatly decorated by compartments coloured in tints resembling an autumnal leaf, the yellow-green of which, forms the pannels, and its mellower and pinky hues compose a very narrow border and stile that surround them. The draperies are of buff chintz, in which sage-green leaves, and small pink and blue-and-white flowers prevail; the furniture is cane-coloured. Upright flower-stands of basket-work are placed in each angle of the room and the verandah is constantly dressed with plants of the choicest scents and colours . . .

The book-room is coloured a tea-green, which is relieved by blossom colour and brown.

The chambers are papered with a small and simple trellis pattern, and the draperies white, with a mixtture of lavender colour and buff.

Burlington Arcade, Piccadilly

Even in more sophisticated houses, much of this simplicity remained. Miss Edgeworth, the novelist and writer of children's books,
visiting Thomas Hope near Dorking in 1819, was vexed by the
obtrusive foreign and classical influence. "This house is magnifi-
cently furnished but to my taste much too fine for a country house
even putting the idea of comfort out of the question. There is too
much Egyptian ornament – Egyptian hieroglyphic figures bronze
and gilt but all hideous . . ." Miss Berry, the diarist, had felt much
the same distaste when in 1811 she had visited the Brighton Pavilion.
"All is Chinese, quite overloaded with china of all sorts and of all
forms, but so overloaded one upon another, that the effect is more
like a china shop baroquement arranged, than the abode of a Prince.
All is gaudy without looking gay; and all is crowded with ornaments,
without being magnificent . . . The riding-house . . . is, I think, likely
not to be finished, though it is the only part of the habitation of the
Prince which deserves preservation."

Yet Miss Berry failed to see that the Pavilion perfectly expressed
the other element of the Regency spirit. There was a pleasing native
simplicity about design; there was also a delightful exuberance, a
Romantic fantasy, a theatrical sense, an intense, endearing gusto,
and of this the Pavilion remains the symbol. In the Pavilion, drawn

from many sources, are the extravaganza which belong to the age of the Regent, the age of Coleridge and Kubla Khan. Under the stately pleasure domes is a concatenation of exorbitant delights. In the corridor stands a games table, its end supports carved with swans' heads and scallop shells. In the banqueting room are a silver-gilt candelabrum of seven lights, its branches chased with lions' masks and birds' heads, and a silver-gilt sideboard dish modelled with swans and bulrushes, and with a rim of shells and bay leaves and a plaque showing Jupiter taking vengeance upon the earth. In the Great Kitchen, where Carême reigned for eight months as the Regent's chef, the pillars are designed as palm trees. In the south drawing-room is the Dolphin Furniture presented to Greenwich Hospital for Seafarers in memory of Nelson. It is richly gilt, and carved with dolphins, acanthus leaves, sphinxes, and cornucopiæ. The harp in the music room is carved with figures of Victory.

In countless portraits, diaries and letters, in contemporary designs, one can see the simple elegance of Regency decoration; but the Pavilion enshrines its jubilant splendour.

IV. FASHION AND PLEASURE

FASHION, like furniture, was both simple and extravagant. During the Regency, men started to wear trousers instead of breeches, and the reign of the tall hat began. Women wore plain muslin dresses, and, even in winter, morning dresses were still made of the same thin material. Dinner dresses were made of velvet and satin, and in about 1812 there was a vogue for velvet dresses trimmed with swansdown. In the evening, gowns were cut square and very low over the bosom. Dresses were trimmed with frills or rolls of the same material, and only in 1812 did dressmakers begin to use different coloured trimmings. The most typical garment of the period was the pelisse. This was a kind of over-dress which buttoned down the front, and it was sometimes made fairly short in order to display a few inches of a white muslin dress underneath. Sometimes it had a double or triple shoulder cape, like a man's box coat. When the weather was severe, a "pilgrim's cloak" was thrown over the pelisse, or furs were worn. Ankle-boots for women made their appearance, and slippers had slashings of contrasting colours. Gold ornaments began to replace the coloured stones which had been in fashion. In the first years of the Regency, white had been the most popular colour; but from about 1814 soft colours appeared. One morning dress in 1813 was "a Polonese robe and petticoat, of fine cambric or jaconet muslin . . . A bonnet-cap, composed of jonquille satin . . . Gloves and

Fashion plates, 1810: (1) Walking and morning dress, (2) Half dress, (3) Full dress, (4) Evening promenade or sea beach costumes

slippers of yellow kid". Carriage dress was "a Russian mantle, of pomona or spring green sarsnet, lined with white satin, and trimmed with rich frog fringe. Slippers of green kid". One delightful evening dress was "a celestial blue satin slip . . . A Polonese long robe of white crape, or gossamer net". The hair was worn "in irregular curls, confined in the Eastern style, and blended with flowers".

The end of the Napoleonic Wars at Waterloo brought a marked change in the shape of women's dresses. The waist rose even higher than it had been before (it did not return to normal level until the 1820s), and the skirt came straight down from the waist to just above the ankles. The bottom of the skirt was, however, much wider and much more decorated, generally with stiff *rouleaux* of material. Women began to wear transparent materials over opaque ones, and it became the fashion to wear a dress of pink crape over a slip of white satin, or a net dress over a slip of coloured satin. Sleeves became elaborate, puckered muslin was used to give them a puffed appearance, and the ruff round the neck emphasised that the Tudor period was in vogue. The influence of Walter Scott was also reflected in the fashion for plaid scarves and sashes in about 1817. Handbags, or reticules, first appeared when clinging muslin dresses were worn, because pockets could no longer be hidden.

The victories of Wellington's armies brought the military into fashion. Military headgear was copied, and frogging and epaulettes added a further patriotic touch. In 1811, carriage costume might be "a military coat or pelisse of amber-coloured velvet . . . Half-boots of amber-coloured kid". In 1813, evening dress might be "richly ornamented, *à la militaire*, with gold braid and netted buttons, forming a sort of epaulette on the shoulders". The Wellington hat, the Wellington bonnet, and even the Wellington jacket were popular.

Fashion footnote: the Wellington boot

The Repository of the Arts advocated "the Vittoria or Wellington costume for evening dress. Hair in dishevelled curls, with variegated laurel band in front". There was also a Wellington mantle. The plain cottage bonnet became more elaborate: it was cut out in front to display a lace cap underneath. Hats became higher and were decorated with flowers, feathers, or puffed gauze. They were worn in the evening, except with full dress, when flowers or feathers were worn. In 1814 a fashion plate showed five delectable head-dresses: a full turban, made in tiffany or silver net; a melon cap, made of quilted white satin; a Persian calash; a cottage bonnet, made in salmon colour and white velvet; and a Russian *à la mode*, made of orange and white velvets.

The author of *The Hermit in London*, a series of sketches published in 1819–20, made some caustic remarks on women's dress:

The same show-room tricks are practised upon our belles, as are played off upon our beaux; and a whole dictionary of strange names is invented, in order to give attraction to the articles of wearing apparel. We have robes *à la Joconde*, and *à la Turque*; we have a head-dress *à la Caroline*, *à la Victime*, *à la Ninon*: we have cottage-bonnets, and curricle-gowns, and

Beau Brummell, perhaps the most celebrated dandy of all time. Left:
Bond Street loungers, 1820

gipsy-hats, and Oldenburgh pokes, and Homburg, or humbug, hats, and
I know not what beside. All this renders the town a complete masquerade,
and makes every drawing-room seem like a stage filled with actresses in
different costumes . . .

If the fair sex would consult a friend instead of a dress-maker, less errors
and less expense would attend their toilette.

Regency dandies were as extravagant as their wives and daughters.
As the Hermit observed:

A distinguished Exquisite is padded all over to-day; and all the other
foplings are, on the morrow, mere walking pin-cushions. A fat prince, or
a fat dandy, requires confinement in his limbs; and all his subjects are
immediately restrained within the same limits . . .

One day, the back is to be as broad as an Irish chairman's, and the
shoulders to be bolstered up to imitate a hod-man; and the next, the
shoulders are to be flat, and a man is to be pinched in and laced up until
he resembles an earwig . . .

All these are Master Snip's manoeuvres, who continues to make his bill
equally long, whether the spencer or the box-coat be in vogue.

The Regent himself could wear the simplest or the most extravagant clothes with consummate ease. He insisted on correct dress, but he felt free to set a fashion. He considered it a want of respect when Captain Gronow, the memoir-writer, appeared in his presence wearing trousers instead of knee-breeches. Within a month, however, the Regent was also wearing black trousers. He remained fascinated by dress: In 1811 Lady Blessington snapped that he had gone "to inspect the cloathing and fancy new Regimentals round the Coast". In 1813, in his *Intercepted Letters*, Tom Moore explained:

> Some monarchs take roundabout ways into note,
> But His short cut to fame is – the cut of his coat!
> Philip's Son thought the World was too small for his Soul,
> While our R – G – T's finds room in a lac'd buttonhole!

In 1818, Moore reported that the Regent had "thought of giving red waistcoats and breeches to the navy". It would have been a pleasant Brummell touch.

Captain Jesse, Brummell's biographer, added his cynical note:

The Prince, not Brummell, was the Mæcenas of tailors; and perhaps no King of England ever wasted so much time on the details of his dress, or devising alterations in that of his troops. On this point he displayed neither taste nor judgment, as the chin of many a Life-Guardsman on a windy day attested . . . The proceeds of the sale of his wardrobe amounts to the enormous sum of fifteen thousand pounds; and if we are to judge by the price of a cloak purchased by Lord Chesterfield for two hundred and twenty, the sable lining alone having originally cost eight hundred, it is scarcely straining the point to suppose that this collection of royal garments had cost little less than one hundred thousand pounds.

The age to which the Regent gave his name was an age for pleasures. There was the undoubted pleasure of dress; there was also the pleasure of eating, and the most spectacular banquets were those devised by Antonin Carême for the Regent himself. Carême wrote a number of books on the art of cooking, and the earliest was *Le pâtissier royal parisien*, published in 1815: the year before he entered the Regent's service. We can imagine these splendid set-pieces, made largely of spun sugar, adorning the tables at Carlton House and the Pavilion, and we can watch Carême supervising their making in the kitchen. Among them is a full-scale replica of a French helmet. "When the helmet, which is of *pâte d'Office*, is fixed upon its stand,

Fashion plates, 1811: (1) Promenade dress, (2) Walking dress, (3) Walking dress or carriage costume, (4) Opera dress

Antonin Carême wrote a number of books on the art of cooking, and he supervised the Royal kitchens. These designs were meant for the banquet table; the *Hermitage suédois* was made from biscuits, the full-scale helmets were created from pastry and spun sugar.

cover it slightly with a brush dipped in clear apricot jam, or quince or apple jelly, to render it brilliant; the horsehair is of deep coloured caramel; the plume is white; the wreath of green biscuits . . ." Beside the French helmet is a Roman helmet with "horsehair" of silver spun sugar, and a laurel wreath cut out of green almond biscuits. There are a harp, a lyre and a globe in spun sugar, a Gothic pavilion and a hermitage on a rock both made of biscuits, not to mention a Turkish cottage and a Turkish mill. "The Turkish Mill is round, of *pâte d'Office* masked with stripes of red and white sugar; the sails of white spun sugar; the rock work is of *croques en bouche*, glazed with light caramel . . ." It was a long way from the splendours of such a table, from the boar's head and champagne, to Mrs Sneyd's middle-class luncheon, described by Maria Edgeworth:

Luncheon – damson pie – pork pie – mutton steaks – hot mashed potatoes – puffs – un-noticed – brawn untouched – cold roast beef on sideboard – seen too late! Observation by Mrs Sneyd – Not well bred ever you know to put the gravy on the meat when you serve any body – No because you should leave the person at liberty to eat it or not as they please – Just like butter on and *off* vegetables it should be – Yes and just like love which you should be allowed to take or leave. With such nonsense as this and much laughter that must appear *causeless* in writing we go on most happily.

Merchants in the City of London went on most happily, too. At The Cock, behind the Royal Exchange, they could enjoy "turtle, gravy, and other soups, excellent dinners, and the best of wines". Five hundred people dined there every day. The Feathers in Hand Court, Holborn, specialised in excellent chops, Burton ale and oysters; and there were "a variety of convenient and cheap houses, called Cooks Shops, scattered over every part of the town, in which a dinner may be had at the low rate of 1s. or 1/6d".

Those who were more concerned with the pleasures of the mind and imagination could delight in music. As that useful guide, *The Picture of London*, explained to its readers in 1813:

Music has rarely held a higher rank among the fashionable amusements of this metropolis, than at the present time . . . First, in the class of composers for the piano-forte, ranks the celebrated Clementi. Pre-eminent, as a female singer, stands the inimitable Billington. Catalini possesses an extraordinary compass, power, and flexibility of voice; her style of execution is peculiar to herself, and its rapidity can hardly be surpassed by a performer on the instrument. [Among the gentlemen singers] Braham continues to receive the applause with which his exertions have been so successfully crowned . . .

In 1819 Richard Rush went to Drury Lane, where "*Guy Mannering* was the play, and 'Scots wha' ha' wi' Wallace bled,' was sung by Braham . . . The song, which breathes the spirit of freedom and heroism, was enthusiastically applauded, and encored twice".

It was a brilliant age for the theatre. Edmund Kean (1787–1833) was one of the greatest English actors of all time. His father is presumed to have been an architect's clerk, and his mother an actress. His childhood and youth were unsettled; he began his career by joining a strolling company of players, and he endured years of hardship and privation. On 26th January, 1814, he appeared upon the stage at Drury Lane: a short, undistinguished and insignificant actor from the provinces. That night, as Shylock, he became the magnet of attraction, and the future prop of the theatre. On his second appearance as Shylock, the receipts at the box-office nearly doubled, and, on 12th February, Drury Lane "literally overflowed in every quarter to witness his Richard III". "I went . . . to the play, to see Kean for the first time," Miss Berry, the diarist, wrote in her journal on 28th March. "It was *Richard III*. It pleased me, but I was not enthusiastic . . . *31st March*. Went to see Kean in *Hamlet*. I must confess I am disappointed in his talent. To my mind he is without grace and elevation of mind . . ." But, whatever Miss Berry's opinion, Kean performed Othello that summer at a gala evening for the Allied Sovereigns; and, during the seasons of 1815, 1816, and 1817, he continued, single-handed, to save Drury Lane from financial collapse. "I saw Kean return to the public in 'Richard III,' and finely he did it," Keats reported late in 1817. Kean enhanced his reputation as Macbeth, but Othello was his masterpiece, and his

The Drury Lane Theatre in 1808

Edmund Kean, shown here as Richard III

third act was the climax of that noble piece of acting. He excelled
as the exponent of passion; and Coleridge declared: "Seeing him
act was like reading Shakespeare by flashes of lightning." Like
many actors after him, Kean understood the value of publicity. At
the height of his fame, he was presented with a tame lion; he was
sometimes found playing with it in his drawing-room.

While Kean ensured the fortunes of Drury Lane Theatre, John
Philip Kemble (1757–1823) ensured the prosperity of Covent
Garden by his management and his acting. In 1813, *The Picture of
London* reported that

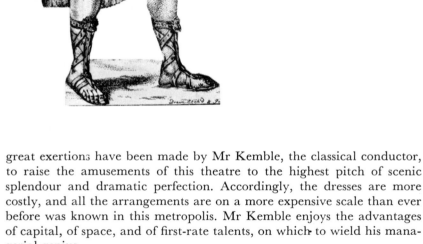

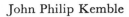
John Philip Kemble

great exertions have been made by Mr Kemble, the classical conductor, to raise the amusements of this theatre to the highest pitch of scenic splendour and dramatic perfection. Accordingly, the dresses are more costly, and all the arrangements are on a more expensive scale than ever before was known in this metropolis. Mr Kemble enjoys the advantages of capital, of space, and of first-rate talents, on which to wield his managerial genius.

The performers are, Messrs. J. and C. Kemble, Young, Munden, Fawcett, Farley, Liston, &c., and Mrs Siddons, Mrs C. Kemble, &c.

John Kemble's tall, imposing figure, his noble features and his grave demeanour were uniquely suited to the Roman characters in Shakespeare's plays. He excelled in declamation, but he could not express vehemence or pathos. He gave his last performance, as Coriolanus, on 23rd June, 1817. The future was none the less secure: in 1816 the young William Charles Macready had made his first triumphant appearance at Covent Garden.

One or two actresses glittered in this brilliant constellation. Among them were Fanny Kelly, beloved of Charles Lamb, and Mrs Jordan (the mistress of the Regent's brother, the Duke of Clarence). But such figures naturally paled beside that of John Kemble's immortal sister.

Mrs Siddons had been a star in the now distant days of George III. She had been received at Buckingham House, she had taught elocution to the Princesses, and she had performed all her parts before the Royal Family. King George III, so she recalled, "was often moved to tears which he as often vainly endeavoured to conceal behind his eye-glass, and her Majesty the Queen, at one time told me in her gracious broken English that her only refuge from me was actually turning her back upon the stage". The highest in the land had always been among her admirers. At the theatre, Sir Joshua Reynolds "always sat in the orchestra, and in that place were to be seen . . . Burke, Gibbon, Sheridan . . .; and these great men would often visit my Dressing Room after the Play, to make their bows and

Sarah Siddons as Catherine of Aragon in Shakespeare's *Henry VIII*. She had been a star since the days of George III.

93

honour me with their applauses. I must repeat O glorious days! Neither did His Royal Highness the Prince of Wales withhold his gracious approbation." He not only applauded her: he later found a position in the East India Company for one of her sons.

Mrs Siddons played all the great rôles of tragedy, but she wisely left comedy alone. Rather taller than average, she had a splendid figure, classical features, large and eloquent eyes, a rich, resonant voice, and impeccable diction. She concentrated on each character she played with such intensity that she seemed to be possessed by it.

When the Regency began, she had reached the zenith of her career; in 1812, at the age of fifty-seven, she decided to retire from the stage. As a critic explained: "Her powers had in no way declined, but her figure had become corpulent and unwieldy; so much so that, latterly, when she knelt to the Duke, as Isabella in *Measure for Measure*, she was unable to rise without assistance." On 29th June, she gave her farewell performance in *Macbeth*. The audience would not let the play proceed beyond the sleepwalking scene, for Lady Macbeth was her finest part, and she performed it to perfection.

Alas, she was persuaded to emerge from retirement, and to give occasional performances. Her reading of *Measure for Measure* in 1813 did not answer Miss Edgeworth's expectation; and, in 1816, Hazlitt gave a sad picture of Mrs Siddons, who had attempted again to play Lady Macbeth.

Mrs Siddons retired once from the stage: why should she return to it again? She cannot retire from it twice with dignity; and yet it is to be wished that she should do all things with dignity . . .

If it was reasonable that Mrs Siddons should retire from the stage three years ago, certainly those reasons have not diminished since, nor do we think Mrs Siddons would consult what is due to her powers or her fame, in commencing a new career . . .

Mrs Siddons always spoke as slow as she ought: she now speaks slower than she did . . . The machinery of the voice seems too ponderous for the power that wields it. There is too long a pause between each sentence, and between each word in each sentence. There is too much preparation. The stage waits for her. In the sleeping scene, she produced a different impression from what we expected. It was more laboured, and less natural. In coming on formerly, her eyes were open, but the sense was shut. She was like a person bewildered, and unconscious of what she did. She moved her lips involuntarily; all her gestures were involuntary and mechanical. At present she acts the part more with a view to effect . . . There was none of this weight or energy in the way she did the scene the first time we saw her, twenty years ago.

Mrs Siddons last performed on 9th July, 1819. She died in 1831.

The Aquatic Theatre, Sadler's Wells, Islington, was "limited to the representation of burlettas, ballets, pantomimes, rope or wire-dancing, tumbling, and other feats of activity."

Those who preferred lighter entertainments in Regency London might visit Sadler's Wells, which was "limited to the representation of burlettas, ballets, pantomimes, rope or wire-dancing, tumbling, and other feats of activity". They might while away a pleasant evening at Vauxhall Gardens. As the guide explained:

These gardens are beautiful and extensive, and contain a variety of walks, brilliantly illuminated with variegated coloured lamps, terminated with transparent paintings . . .

The grove is beautifully illuminated in the evening with about fifteen thousand glass lamps, which glitter among the trees, and produce a brilliant effect . . .

From 5,000 to 16,000 well-dressed persons are occasionally present.

People did not simply seek public entertainment. Since there were no mass media, they created entertainment for themselves. They painted, embroidered, played musical instruments, and they delighted in the diverse pleasures of collecting. Foreign visitors were at times surprised by this collectors' mania. Richard Rush, the American Minister, visited Lord Castlereagh at his country seat, North Cray, in Kent, and inspected the menagerie. It led him to make some observations on English taste.

Taste, in England, appears to take every form. In this receptacle, were lions, ostriches, kangaroos, and I know not what variety of strange animals. Those who collect rare books and pictures, are too numerous to be computed; so,

95

Vauxhall Gardens

A visitor to Regency London might spend an instructive afternoon at the Royal Menagerie or Bullocks Museum.

those who gather relics and curiosities from all parts of the world. Some persons are conchologists; they have the shells of all coasts arranged under scientific classification, like plants in botany. Some collect *pipes* (although not smoking them), from the beaded patterns of the Mohawks, to those of Persia and Constantinople studded with jewels and gold; on the gratification of this taste, I am told of an individual who had actually laid out £7000 sterling. And here, amidst lawns and gardens, amidst all that denoted cultivation and art, I beheld wild beasts and outlandish birds – the tenants of uncivilised forests and skies – set down as if for contrast!

Visitors of less distinction might not inspect Lord Castlereagh's menagerie; but they visited Bullock's Museum in Piccadilly, which contained "upwards of ten thousand different articles, including quadrupeds, birds, reptiles, insects, ancient arms, works of art, etc." This exhibition must have been closely rivalled by Polito's

Choosing fabrics at the shop of Messrs Harding, Howell & Co., Pall Mall

Living Museum in the Strand. It housed "a collection of divers living beasts and birds, which are not even exceeded in variety by those of the royal menagerie in the Tower". They included a royal tiger from Bengal, and five "kanguroos". At Wigley's Royal Promenade Rooms, in Spring Gardens, the exhibition included "a panoramic view of St Petersburgh; an invisible girl, who will speak or sing at the desire of the spectator; a young Albiness, with silver-coloured hair; and thirty panoramic views of foreign cities and sea pieces. Mr Maillardet's automatical exhibition is in these rooms, and contains, among various other curiosities, many pieces of superior mechanism; a female figure who plays on the harpsichord, a small figure that dances on the tightrope, and a bird which admirably imitates the notes of nature." At the Linwood Gallery, in Leicester Square, were Miss Linwood's needlework copies of famous paintings.

Those who were seriously interested in art had unrivalled facilities to indulge their interest. "For the fine arts," as the guide explained in 1813, "London is now much and deservedly distinguished. The commotions on the continent have operated as a hurricane on the productions of genius, and the finest works of ancient and modern times have been removed from their old situations. Many, very many of them . . . are now in the private collections of our nobility and gentry, in and about the metropolis." Several of these collections were open to the public; and, at the Royal Academy Schools, Mr Fuseli, the professor in painting, delivered six lectures during the winter season. Mr Soane, the professor in architecture, delivered a course on his subject. Mr Turner lectured on perspective.

V. REGENCY ART

THE REGENCY was a fruitful age for painting, but the artist who best caught its spirit was Sir Thomas Lawrence, the foremost portrait-painter of the day. He was born in 1769, in Bristol, where his father was the innkeeper of the White Lion. Four years after the child's birth, Mr Lawrence moved to the Black Bear at Devizes, and there the boy won a reputation as a prodigy with his pencil portraits. In 1782, when his family moved to Bath, Lawrence set up professionally. He had little regular education or artistic training, and he did not begin to practise in oils until he moved to London in 1786. He studied briefly at the Royal Academy schools, where he was encouraged by Reynolds. His early success was phenomenal, and when he was twenty he was summoned to Windsor Castle to paint Queen Charlotte. After the death of Reynolds in 1792, he became the portrait painter of the day.

After the death of John Hoppner in 1810, Lawrence was patronised by the Prince Regent. In an age of rigid class distinction, when every Exclusive shrank from contact with a Nobody, the Regent showed not only his taste and his munificence, he was charmingly accessible. Miss Croft, a friend of Lawrence's, remembered how the artist was painting a portrait of the Duchess of Gloucester. She had dressed a lay figure in his studio in white satin and the Duchess's jewels, but they had been unable to get on her wig. The Regent and a friend chose this moment to call at the studio.

The Regent entered first, but instantly started back on seeing the bald-headed lady, and Sir Thomas had much trouble to persuade him that the lady was perfectly indifferent to the state in which he had surprised her. The Prince and the other two then tried their united efforts, but the wig baffled their endeavours as it had done mine . . .

Another day George IV [as the Regent became] caused us a great fright; he always went to Sir Thomas to sit, with his usual condescension, while he was Regent, but it was no longer etiquette when he came to the throne. One day a friend of mine was sitting, and we were a party of five or six, the rooms strewed with bonnets, cloaks and draperies of all sorts, when a message came that the Regent would be with him at three o'clock. He therefore broke up the sitting and ordered coffee, which I was in the act of pouring out, when a dreadful knocking was heard at the street door, and Sir Thomas flew to receive his royal guest, leaving us to scamper off as we could . . . We made our escape by the back stairs just before the Regent entered the room we had quitted. "Lawrence," he said, "it is my fate to disturb your family, for here is even the coffee poured out and not drunk." Sir Thomas then explained that we were only a group of terrified sitters.

Lawrence's first portrait of the Regent was exhibited in 1815. That year, the Regent knighted him, and commissioned him to

John Constable (self-portrait)

paint the first of the portraits of allied heads of state and military leaders for the Royal collection at Windsor. In 1818 the Regent sent him to the Continent to continue his series of portraits. While Lawrence was still at work at Aix-la-Chapelle, he received his patron's commands,

as a completion of the general plan, to proceed to Rome, to paint for him the Pope and Cardinal Gonsalvi. I have no doubt [he told a friend] that almost a principal motive with His Royal Highness was, the desire to terminate my mission in the most gratifying manner to myself, with an addition of honour, and of one of the highest enjoyments that an artist could be supposed to taste.

Lawrence duly went to Rome, and "was honoured with an audience of the Pope, at the Quirinal Palace . . . With a phrase or two of French (which he does not like to speak), and the rest in Italian, he spoke his sense of the Prince Regent's attention to him, and his gladness to satisfy his wish." Lawrence's portrait of Pius VII was his masterpiece. He followed it with a portrait of Cardinal Gonsalvi, "one of the finest subjects for a picture that I have ever had". On his return to England in 1820, Lawrence was elected President of the Royal Academy in succession to Benjamin West. He died in London ten years later.

He had been not only an artist, but a connoisseur. His collection of old master drawings was remarkable, and he had been instrumental in securing the Elgin Marbles for the nation and in founding the National Gallery. As for his portraits, they had established him as the first portrait painter of Europe – indeed, he stimulated French painting almost as effectively as Constable. His portraits do not merely record the famous faces and the elegant fashions of the Regency: they catch its epic, dramatic quality, its confidence and splendour.

Just as Lawrence dominated the portrait-painting of the age, so John Constable (1776–1837) stood out as the leading painter of landscape – not only during the Regency, but perhaps in all the history of English art. He was born at East Bergholt, Suffolk, the son of a wealthy miller. He was originally intended for the Church, but while he was still at school he began to take an interest in landscape painting. In about 1793 he left school to work for his father; and he could not finally leave his father's counting-house to follow his vocation until 1799, when he was listed as a probationer at the Royal Academy schools. In 1800 he became a full student. His development was slow, but he was largely self-taught, and he had to earn some of his living by portraiture.

In 1811 he exhibited "Dedham Vale" at the Royal Academy: an ambitious panorama of the Essex countryside seen at noon on a summer day. It was a significant year in his life, for he also fell in love with Maria Bicknell. He was not allowed to marry her until 1816, when at last he had financial security. From 1811 to 1826 he pursued his solitary path, seeking how best to record the English landscape and its transient moods. "There is," he said, "room in this country for a *natural* painter." The evidence of his search remains in over 300 drawings and oil studies now at the Victoria and Albert Museum.

In 1815 he showed his "Boat-building" at the Royal Academy, and in 1817 he showed "Flatford Mill". The French were the first to acclaim him publicly, when he exhibited three at the paintings Salon of 1824. Delacroix, who saw them, repainted the background of one of his own pictures. Constable liberated French landscape artists from the weight of tradition. He did not calculate picturesque effects: he presented nature with humility and sincerity. He was the first landscape painter to recognise the importance of the momentary

Constable's "Flatford Mill from Lock on Stour", painted about 1811

and spontaneous impression, and to preserve it in his paintings. He was never at ease when he moved far from Suffolk: he was parochial, and made a virtue of it. But, as John Piper wrote, "he made the contrasted sparkle and gloom of nature in a small part of one county stand as a symbol for the sparkle and gloom of the world and of eternity".

Constable saw reality with his own eyes. Joseph Mallord William Turner saw it with his imagination. He was moved by "the Weather in our Souls". He was born in London in 1775, the son of a barber, and at the age of ten he was sent to live with an uncle at Brentford, Middlesex, where he went to school. He entered the Royal Academy schools in 1789, and exhibited a watercolour the following year, when he was a boy of fifteen. From 1796 he began to exhibit oils as well as watercolours at the Academy. In his summer holidays he travelled considerably, making sketches which he later developed.

J. M. W. Turner (from the portrait by John Philip)

By the turn of the century, his career was assured, and in 1802 he became a Royal Academician. He never married, and he was so determined to paint undisturbed that he became secretive about where he lived. He lived in Hammersmith and then at Twickenham. Among the famous pictures which he painted during the Regency were "Dido Burning Carthage" (1815), which he bequeathed to the National Gallery; "Oxford" (1811); "Frosty Morning" (1813); and – one of his most ambitious canvases – "England: Richmond Hill, on the Prince Regent's Birthday" (1819). This is now in the Tate Gallery.

Turner was a pioneer in the study of light, colour and atmosphere, and here he anticipated the French Impressionists. He painted veiled light, misty light, full light or blinding light. Hazlitt wrote of his pictures: "They are pictures of the elements of air, earth and water. The artist delights to go back to the first chaos of the world." Constable had expressed his own experience of nature; Turner recreated it from his imagination. He did not distinguish reality from the pictures which he created to reflect his dreams. He lived on until 1851, into the unromantic Victorian age, but he remains a romantic and, above all, a visionary.

The England of his day had other visionaries. Henry Fuseli (1741–1825) painted fantasies with what Coleridge called "vigorous impotence". John Martin (1789–1854) illustrated Milton's *Paradise Lost*, and showed a sombre, splendid, and entirely Romantic imagination. But the visionary who towered above them both was William Blake (1757–1827). Poet, painter and seer, he was the son of a London hosier. In time he was to describe the visionary experiences he had had as a child: once he had seen angels in a tree at Peckham Rye. He wanted to be an artist, and at the age of ten he began to attend a drawing school. He educated himself by reading and by the study of engravings from paintings by Renaissance masters. In 1772 he was apprenticed to an engraver. When he finished his apprenticeship in 1779 he entered the Royal Academy schools as an engraving student. While he was there he earned his keep by engraving for publishers, and he also produced watercolours. He married in 1782, and there followed an astonishing outburst of creative activity: among his works were his first masterpieces:

An illustration by William Blake for the Book of Job. Blake was hardly a typical Regency figure; his visions would have left their mystical impression on any age.

"Hannibal Crossing the Alps": a picture painted by Turner during the Regency

Songs of Innocence and *The Book of Thel* (both engraved in 1789). *Songs of Innocence* was the first complete book executed by Blake by his new method of illuminated printing. The text and designs were etched in relief on copper, and the prints from these plates were then illuminated by hand. In 1794 *Songs of Experience* were added to *Songs of Innocence*. "I find more & more," Blake told a friend, "that my Style of Designing is a Species by itself, & in this which I send you I have been compell'd by Genius or Angel to follow where he led; if I were to act otherwise it would not fulfil the purpose for which alone I live." Blake's long period of obscurity coincided roughly with the Regency. But his influence was already felt. He created work composed of a strange array of elements: medieval art, the Bible, Milton and Shakespeare, Dante. He was the most mystic of English painters.

The Regency – so romantic in its architecture and poetry, was also the age for Romantic art. David Cox (1783–1859) worked as a scene-painter in his youth, and scene-painting affected him for a long while. His canvases have an open-air vitality about them, and he produced fine effects of light and season. The greatest of the later topographical and archaeological artists was John Sell Cotman (1782–1842); his watercolours made him the pre-eminent member of the Norwich School. Another leading member of the school was John Crome (1768–1821), often called Old Crome to distinguish him from his son. Crome was born in Norwich, the son of a weaver, and he first exhibited at the Royal Academy in 1806. He took his subjects almost entirely from Norfolk scenery, and he presented them in a manner largely influenced by his study of Dutch painters. Samuel Prout, the watercolourist (1783–1852), was born in Plymouth. In 1813 he published *The Rudiments of Landscape, with Progressive Studies,* the first of his handbooks for art students. In 1819 a visit to France distinguished him from earlier English topographers: he chose foreign townscapes as his subjects. Prout showed skill in composition, and a flair for seeing the picturesque.

Two further artists must be mentioned. Thomas Rowlandson (1756–1827) was born in London, the son of a tradesman or City merchant. He studied at the Royal Academy schools and in Paris. He was largely employed by Rudolph Ackermann, the art publisher. Ackermann brought the art of the aquatint to its highest perfection in England, and he was among the first to see the possibilities of lithography. In 1809–11 Ackermann issued in his *Poetical Magazine* "The Schoolmaster's Tour" – a series of plates which became highly popular. These were again engraved by Rowlandson himself in 1812, and issued under the title of the *Tour of Dr Syntax in Search of the Picturesque.* The work had reached a fifth edition by 1813. Row-

One of Thomas Rowlandson's drawings from *The Tour of Dr Syntax*

landson was one of the masters of caricature. His designs were usually drawn with a reed pen and delicately washed in colour. Then they were etched by the artist on copper and afterwards aquatinted.

Thomas Bewick (1753–1828) was credited with reviving the art of wood-engraving in England. Certainly he is its Past Grand Master. He introduced a technique of illustration, and inspired a school whose best work remains unsurpassed. Bewick was born in Northumberland. His master (later his partner) was Ralph Beilby, an engraver who did much work for the Newcastle silversmiths. Bewick

showed remarkable talent as a wood engraver, and he published several popular illustrated works. His *General History of Quadrupeds* appeared in 1790; his most famous publication was his *History of British Birds* (*Land Birds*, 1797; *Water Birds*, 1804). This ran to many editions, not only during the Regency, but for years afterwards. "A good naturalist cannot be a bad man." That is the self-portrait of Bewick, drawn in the preface to his work on birds. Bewick is a good naturalist, and (as his *Memoir* shows) a good man; he is a downright Romantic, but he is that rare and blessed creature, a Romantic with

Left: Thomas Bewick in his studio. Above: an engraving of a nightingale
from his *History of British Birds*

a sense of humour. He is not afraid of the crude in his pictures or
in his prose; he does show a broad love and a real understanding of
all nature. Such is our admiration of his engraving, that Bewick's
writing has been overshadowed, if not forgotten. But how carefully
he decides that the Godwit's head is "a dingy reddish pale brown"!
How finely he speaks of his favourite Goosander, whose "legs and
feet are deep scarlet, like sealing-wax"! As for his engravings, they
remain not only a faithful record of nature, but a robust, endearing
and accurate impression of rustic life in Regency days.

One sculptor dominates the Regency: Francis Legatt Chantrey. He
was born near Sheffield in 1781. His father, a carpenter, died when
the boy was twelve, and young Chantrey had to begin life as a wage-
earner in a grocer's shop. In his sixteenth year he was apprenticed to
a carver and gilder in Sheffield. Wood-carving whetted his appetite,
and he experimented with pencils and clay, and took lessons in
chalk portraiture. Other friends taught him how to use a mallet and
chisel on marble and stone, and they instructed him in the art of
painting. In 1802, he cancelled his indentures and advertised himself
as a portraitist in crayons. He went to try his fortune in Dublin and
Edinburgh, and in London, where he attended the Royal Academy

Sir Francis Chantrey (a self-portrait) and his statue of George IV – the former Regent – at Brighton

schools. His first commission for sculpture came in 1805, but it was only in 1811 that his bust of Horne Tooke was exhibited at the Royal Academy, and brought him fortune and celebrity. In 1818 he was elected a Royal Academician, and in 1835 he was knighted. He died in 1841, leaving his fortune to his widow, and after her death to the Royal Academy. Most of the income from the bequest was to be spent on buying the most valuable works of sculpture and painting by artists of any nation living in Great Britain at the time of execution.

Chantrey produced many busts, but the finest is that of Sir Walter Scott, at Abbotsford. Among his most important statues are those of George IV in Windsor Castle, at Brighton, and in Trafalgar Square. Chantrey's biographer records:

When George IV was sitting to Chantrey, he required the sculptor to give him the idea of an equestrian statue to commemorate him, which Chantrey accomplished at a succeeding interview, by placing in the Sovereign's hand a number of small equestrian figures, drawn carefully on thick paper, and resembling in number and material a pack of cards; these sketches pleased the King very much, who turned them over and over, expressing his surprise that such a variety could be produced; and after a thousand fluctuations of opinion, sometimes for a prancing steed, sometimes for a trotter, then for a neighing or a starting charger, His Majesty at length resolved on a horse standing still as the most dignified for a king. Chantrey probably led to this, as he was decidedly in favour of the four legs being on the ground; he had a quiet and reasonable manner of convincing persons of the propriety of that, which from reflection he judged to be preferable . . .

When he had executed and erected the statue of George IV, on the [Grand] Staircase at Windsor, the King good-naturedly patted the sculptor on the shoulder, and said, "Chantrey, I have reason to be obliged to you, for you have immortalised me."

William Wordsworth, pastoral and philosophical poet. Hazlitt wrote of him: "The tall rock lifts its head in the erectness of his spirit; the cataract roars in the sound of his verse."

VI. REGENCY LITERATURE

DURING THE REGENCY, English poetry reached a brilliance which it had not known since the days of Queen Elizabeth.

William Wordsworth (1770–1850) was not yet elected Poet Laureate. When the Regency began, it was thirteen years since he had published the *Lyrical Ballads*, and in his greatest single poem, *Ode: Intimations of Immortality*, which he finished in 1805–6, he had lamented the passing of inspiration, of the "visionary gleam". *The Prelude* was not to be published until after his death. During the years of the Regency, he remained in his native North of England: a silent presence, but already an influence. He was "Nature's Priest": a pastoral poet enamoured of the English landscape: the majestic Lakes, the gentler West Country, and, no less, of London itself, as seen from Westminster Bridge on a summer day. He was no mere descriptive poet, but a philosopher who was moved by nature, "a dedicated Spirit" who looked in everything for evidence of the existence and purpose of God. In 1812 he told Crabb Robinson, the diarist, "that if men are to become better and wiser, the poems will sooner or later find their admirers". For many readers, he provided a new approach to religious experience.

Wordsworth's friend and contemporary, Samuel Taylor Coleridge (1772–1834), was another brooding presence in the days of the Regency. Poet and lecturer, journalist, critic of literature, theology, philosophy and society, he had one of the most comprehensive minds, one of the most active imaginations of his time. He had been born at Ottery St Mary, in Devon, the youngest of ten children. His father was the headmaster of the local school, and he later became the local vicar. In his ninth year, Coleridge went to school: he entered Christ's Hospital (where he became friends with Charles Lamb); in 1791 he went to Jesus College, Cambridge, where he earned a reputation for his conversation, and for his searching interest in contemporary thought. He went down in 1794 without taking a degree, and in his last Long Vacation he met Robert Southey. They were both poets, both idealists, and together they planned to found a utopian community on the banks of the Susquehanna River in America.

In 1795 Coleridge married Sara Fricker, sister of the future Mrs Southey; and that year came his momentous meeting with Wordsworth. Henceforward Coleridge was torn by conflicting needs: by creative urge and domestic duty. In 1798 he and Wordsworth published the *Lyrical Ballads*; but Coleridge continued to lead an uncertain life. He became leader-writer for the *Morning Post*, he stayed in Malta and Italy, and he remained unhappy, for he constantly compared his own situation with Wordsworth's personal happiness and increasing poetical power. The years 1806–16 were years of depression. Coleridge became addicted to opium (sometimes, reported Southey, "he swallowed a pint a day"). But in April 1816 he settled at Highgate; and, spurred on by his friends, he published a series of notable works, including *Christabel* (1816) which went into three editions. "Coleridge is printing Xtabel," so Charles Lamb told Wordsworth, "by Ld Byron's recommendation to Murray, with what he calls a vision Kubla Khan – which said vision he repeats so enchantingly that it irradiates and brings heaven and Elysian bowers into my parlour while he sings or says it."

> In Xanadu did Kubla Khan
> A stately pleasure-dome decree:
> Where Alph, the sacred river, ran
> Through caverns measureless to man
>   Down to a sunless sea.
> So twice five miles of fertile ground
> With walls and towers were girdled round:
> And there were gardens bright with sinuous rills
> Where blossom'd many an incense-bearing tree;
> And here were forests ancient as the hills,
> Enfolding sunny spots of greenery . . .

The four first rhymes are Southey's, every line:
For God's sake, reader! take them not for mine.

Don Juan was to be Byron's masterpiece. "Almost all *Don Juan* is
real life, either my own, or from people I knew," he told his publisher.
But the poem largely transcended personal feelings.

In October, 1819, Byron presented Moore with the manuscript of
his memoirs, and Moore sold it to Murray for two thousand guineas.
Alas, on the insistence of Murray, and of John Cam Hobhouse, the
poet's friend, it was burned after Byron's death. He died of fever on
19th April, 1824, fighting to liberate Greece from Turkish rule.

And here, perhaps, in brackets, one must mention Robert Southey.
Connected by marriage with Coleridge, satirised by Byron, scorned
by Hazlitt, he was Poet Laureate for most of the Regency. He was
born in Bristol in 1774, and educated at Westminster and at Balliol
College, Oxford. He studied law, travelled in Spain and Portugal,
published his impressions of both, some poems, and a *History of
Brazil*. In 1813 he published a *Life of Nelson*. That year, on the death
of Henry Pye, the Poet Laureateship fell vacant; Walter Scott
declined it, and suggested that it was offered to Southey. "The
whole net income is little more or less than £90," Southey wrote to
Scott. "It comes to me as a God-send." He needed financial support
for his family; he also enjoyed the trappings of office, and his
pompousness led Hazlitt to say of one of his poems: "Every senti-
ment or feeling that he has is nothing but the effervescence of in-
corrigible over-weening self-opinion." In 1816 Southey published
The Poet's Pilgrimage to Waterloo. In 1821, in his *Vision of Judgment*, he
attacked Byron and the Satanic school of poetry – and prompted
Byron's devastating satire of the same name. Henceforward, Southey
wrote mostly prose. He died in 1843, and Wordsworth succeeded
him as Laureate.

If Southey was conventional, the same could not be said of
Thomas Moore. He was born in 1779, the son of a Dublin grocer.
He studied law in Dublin before, in 1799, he paid his first visit to
London, and arranged to publish his translation of the *Odes* of
Anacreon. On his second visit, later that year, he was hailed as
"Anacreon Moore", and welcomed by the patrician Whig families.
He revelled in "the whirl of lords and ladies", as he called it, for he
was an inveterate social climber. In 1801 he published his first book
of lyrics. He enjoyed not only success but patronage and was
recommended for a position in the Court of Admiralty which then

helped to govern Bermuda. He sailed there in 1803, duly feasted on turtle soup and Madeira, and returned home by way of America. Two years after his return to England he published *Epistles, Odes and Other Poems*. This was followed by *Irish Melodies, Intercepted Letters*, and, in 1817, by *Lalla Rookh*, his vastly popular Oriental romance. In 1829 he published his chief prose work, the *Letters and Journals of Lord Byron*. He died in 1852. His fame as a poet lasted his lifetime, but he remains an accomplished writer of words for music. As he predicted: "I shall still have my fame in the *lyrical* way to retire upon."

Moore was a minor poet; Percy Bysshe Shelley was one of the luminaries of English Romantic poetry. He was born in 1792, at Field Place, near Horsham, in Sussex, the son and heir of Timothy Shelley, Conservative Member of Parliament for Shoreham, and the grandson of Sir Bysshe Shelley, baronet. Even as a child he showed subtle feelings and an original mind. In 1804 he went to Eton, and before he left school he published *Zastrozzi: a Romance*, an early attempt at a Gothic romance in the style of Mrs Radcliffe. In the same year, 1810, he also published *Original Poetry by Victor and Cazire*, written with his favourite sister, Elizabeth. That autumn he went up to University College, Oxford, but his stay there was unusually brief. The following March he circulated a pamphlet to the bishops and heads of colleges. It was called *The Necessity of Atheism*. He was inquiring into religion, rather than denying it, but he was immediately sent down.

Before he left Oxford, Shelley had met Harriet Westbrook. She was the daughter of a retired hotelkeeper, and a schoolfriend of his sisters. She became to him the symbol of love and beauty. Five months after he was sent down, he eloped with her to Edinburgh, where they were married. Harriet threw herself eagerly into his dreams of social and political reform (among them the emancipation of Ireland). During the years 1811–12 they moved happily round the British Isles, and the memorial to these years is *Queen Mab*, which Shelley finished in 1812. It was his first major poem. But Harriet was not enough to satisfy him for ever. In March, 1814, he met Mary Godwin. She was the daughter of William Godwin, the philosopher and novelist, and Mary Wollstonecraft. She had the intellectual grasp which Harriet had lacked, and she became the new woman-symbol. Harriet was forgotten, and Shelley and Mary eloped to the Continent.

That autumn they returned to London, where Timothy Shelley

Percy Bysshe Shelley in Rome. A magnificent lyrical poet, Shelley was driven by his quest for intellectual beauty, and by his progressive political and philosophical thought.

decided to allow his son £1,000 a year. But Shelley could not accept a conventional life. There followed more travels in Europe. In 1817, Crabb Robinson met him in London and found his conversation "vehement and arrogant and intolerant". Not long before, the Lord Chancellor had decided that he was unfit to have custody of his children by Harriet, and in March 1818 he and Mary left England for ever. Much of the Shelley of 1818–19 went into *Prometheus Unbound*. The philosophical verse-drama was published in 1820. The hero is a reformer; he is persecuted by the rulers of the universe for trying to improve the lot of humankind.

> To suffer woes which Hope thinks infinite;
> To forgive wrōngs darker than death or night;
>   To defy Power, which seems omnipotent;
> To love, and bear; to hope till Hope creates

From its own wreck the thing it contemplates;
  Neither to change, nor faulter, nor repent;
This, like thy glory, Titan, is to be
Good, great and joyous, beautiful and free;
This is alone Life, Joy, Empire and Victory.

Shelley was drowned on 8th July, 1822, sailing off Leghorn. His body was cremated on the shore in the presence of Leigh Hunt and Byron. Shelley's lyrics have influenced many poets; but he also saw himself as a social reformer. His influence was felt by reformers for generations to come.

One of Shelley's final poems was *Adonais*: an elegy on the death of the most gifted Romantic poet. John Keats had none of the social privilege of Shelley and Byron, none of the educational advantages of Wordsworth and Coleridge. But his achievement was miraculous, and in his promise he outsoared them all.

He was born in 1795, at Moorfields, in London. His father was a groom; his mother's father owned a livery stables. Mr Keats died prematurely, in a riding accident. Mrs Keats died when her son was still a boy. Keats was educated at a school in Enfield, and then – for it seemed a safe career – he was apprenticed to an apothecary, and entered Guy's Hospital, in London, to train as a surgeon. But poetry had already claimed him. He abandoned medicine, and in 1817 he published his first book of poems.

It was dedicated to Leigh Hunt, poet, journalist, critic (and libeller of the Prince Regent). Hunt's cottage in the Vale of Health, at Hampstead, became for Keats a place of pilgrimage. In 1818 there appeared *Endymion*: the tale of the shepherd who fell in love with the moon. The poem was harshly reviewed, but – whatever legend said – Keats was not affected by the criticism. However, the year 1818 was momentous in his life. His married brother George had emigrated to America, his brother Tom died of consumption. Keats found himself alone, and went to live with a genial and devoted friend: a businessman and man of letters, Charles Armitage Brown. That December he moved into Wentworth Place: the stuccoed house in Hampstead which became part of his life and his legend. That autumn, too, he met Fanny Brawne: gay, elegant and eighteen, and he fell utterly in love with her. On Christmas Day they became unofficially engaged.

Soon afterwards, at Chichester, Keats wrote "a little poem call'd 'St Agnes Eve' ". That spring, with her family, Fanny moved into the other half of Wentworth Place. There followed the months in

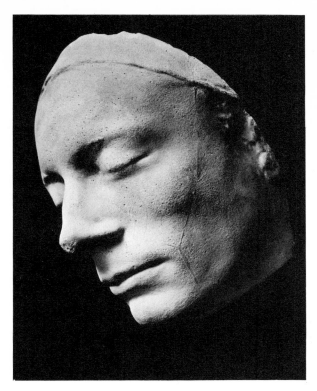

John Keats. From a life-mask. "I think I shall be among the English poets after my death." So Keats surmised. He died at the age of twenty-five, on the threshold of his achievement. He was already the supreme Romantic poet, and one of the finest letter-writers in the English language.

which he wrote with breathtaking prodigality. The *Ode to a Nightingale* was the work of a Hampstead morning: written under a plumtree in the garden. In a letter to his brother in America, he tossed off the *Ode to Psyche, La Belle Dame Sans Merci*, six sonnets, a *Chorus of Faeries*, a pastiche of Spenser, and a little light-hearted extempore. There followed the *Ode on a Grecian Urn*; that summer he was working on *Lamia*, and collaborated with Charles Brown on a drama, *Otho the Great*, and began a drama of his own, *King Stephen*. His *Ode to Autumn* was written at Winchester in September. Driven by love of Fanny Brawne, urged on by financial need, he was also claimed by consumption. In February, 1820, he had the haemorrhage which he recognised as his death warrant; that September – soon after the publication of his third and last book of poems – he left for Italy. As he sailed past the Dorset coast, he wrote his farewell to poetry.

> Bright star! would I were steadfast as thou art –
> Not in lone splendour hung aloft the night,
> And watching, with eternal lids apart,

Like nature's patient, sleepless Eremite,
The moving waters at their priestlike task
    Of pure ablution round earth's human shores,
Or gazing on the new soft fallen mask
    Of snow upon the mountains and the moors –
No – yet still steadfast, still unchangeable,
    Pillow'd upon my fair love's ripening breast,
To feel for ever its soft fall and swell,
    Awake for ever in a sweet unrest,
Still, still to hear her tender-taken breath,
And so live ever – or else swoon to death.

Keats died in Rome on 23rd February, 1821. His letters – which are among the finest in the English language – show his humanity, his humour, his mature and swiftly developing intellect. They reflect his beliefs and progress and his workings as a poet. With the humility of greatness, he had surmised that he might be remembered. "I think I shall be among the English poets after my death." Robert Bridges, years later, answered: "He is. He is, with Shakespeare."

The age of the Romantic poets was also the age of Sir Walter Scott (1771–1832): the first British novelist to become a public figure. He was born in Edinburgh, the son of a solicitor. While he was still an infant, he had an attack of poliomyelitis, and it left him permanently lame. This may have been one reason why, as a child, he read "ten times the usual quantity of fairy tales, eastern stories, romances, &c". In 1783 he matriculated at the Old College of Edinburgh. In 1786 he began his five-year legal apprenticeship with his father, and in 1792 he qualified as an advocate. Five years later, he married: his marriage was one of affection rather than love. In 1805 he published a full-length narrative poem, *The Lay of the Last Minstrel*. It was followed by *Marmion* (1808), *The Lady of the Lake* (1810), *Rokeby* (1813), and *The Lord of the Isles* (1815).

Scott had established himself as a poet, but he was to earn his enduring fame as a novelist. In the autumn of 1813 he had accidentally come across the unfinished manuscript of a novel, *Waverley*. He completed it, and it was published anonymously in 1814. Scott kept his anonymity because he felt that it was improper for a clerk of session to write novels. It must also be said that the mystery gave his novels added glamour, and he understood the value of publicity.

The author of The Waverley Novels. Sir Walter Scott, from the portrait by Sir Edwin Landseer

But the secret was well kept. When David Wilkie was painting the portraits of Scott's family, the eldest daughter told him: "We never have seen a single scrap of the manuscript of any of these novels; but still we have *one* reason for thinking them his: they are the only works published in Scotland of which copies are not presented to Papa." Scott did not confess his authorship until 1827.

Meanwhile, throughout the Regency, the Waverley Novels continued to appear. *Waverley* was followed by *Guy Mannering* (1815); *The Antiquary* (1816); two series of *Tales of My Landlord* (1816–19), which included *Old Mortality* and *The Heart of Midlothian*; *Rob Roy* (1818); and a third series of *Tales of My Landlord*, including *The Bride of Lammermoor* and *The Legend of Montrose* (1819). When he had written these novels of Scottish history, Scott turned to themes from English history. He was driven by financial need, and by the need to satisfy the public appetite for historical fiction which he had created. Henceforward his achievement lay outside the Regency. Early in 1820, George IV conferred a baronetcy on him, and assured him: "I shall always reflect with pleasure on Sir Walter Scott's having been the first creation of my reign."

To modern readers, the Waverley Novels are too long, too detailed and too complex. The time for novels of several hundred pages has passed. But Scott created memorable characters, their authentic background and ambiance, and, at his best, he told a splendid tale. His cult of the Stuart dynasty, his love of Scottish history, his devotion to his native land: these, like his constant need for money, drove him on. As a man, he was pompous, egotistic, sometimes hypocritical, and he was all too clearly an opportunist. But his literary achievement was massive. With a meticulousness and an energy which anticipated those of Dickens and Balzac, he created the historical novel. He also invented the tourist's view of Scotland. His achievements were not always appreciated. "Sir Walter Scott," wrote an angry Scotsman, "has ridiculously made us appear to be a nation of Highlanders, and the bagpipe and the tartan are the order of the day."

If the works of Scott are at times unwieldy, the same could not be said of those of Jane Austen. She was the second daughter of George Austen, rector of the parishes of Steventon and Deane, in Hampshire; she was born at Steventon Parsonage in 1775, and it remained her home for the first 26 years of her life. In 1801 her father resigned his duties, and retired to Bath, where he later died. Only in 1809, when his third son, Edward, gave his mother and sisters a home on his estate at Chawton, did they again have a house of their own. Chawton was Jane Austen's home until she went to Winchester in May, 1817, in search of medical attention. She died there on 18th July, and she was buried in the cathedral.

"Three or four families in a country village," she observed contentedly, "is the very thing to work on." In 1795 she completed the first version of *Sense and Sensibility*. In 1796–7 she wrote the first version of *Pride and Prejudice*. In 1798–9 she wrote *Northanger Abbey*. When she settled at Chawton, she therefore had the manuscripts of three finished novels, and before her first published work appeared, she was already engaged on one of the novels of her maturity. *Mansfield Park* was begun in February, 1811, and *Sense and Sensibility* was published that November. *Pride and Prejudice* appeared in January, 1813. Maria Edgeworth perused it eagerly in her carriage as she drove to London, and Crabb Robinson sat up till the small hours, on successive nights, reading it with admiration. *Emma* was begun in January, 1814, and *Mansfield Park* appeared that May. In the summer of 1815, Jane Austen began *Persuasion*, and that December she published *Emma* – which Tom Moore found "the very per-

Jane Austen, author of *Pride and Prejudice*. Drawn from life by her sister Cassandra

fection of novel-writing". In August, 1816, she finished *Pride and Prejudice*, and between January and March 1817 she was working on the fragment we know as *Sanditon*.

Scott had painted vast panoramas. Miss Austen – as one must call her – drew upper-middle-class life in the English provinces: the hopes and intrigues and pleasures and disappointments of the limited class which she knew. She knew them intimately, she considered them with devastating shrewdness. She described them with humour, compassion, occasional tartness, and with inevitable accuracy. The Regent was her chief admirer. Posterity admires the English understatement of her style, the brilliance of her characters and dialogue, the authentic portrayal of a stratum of Regency society.

Jane Austen concerned herself with the present. Charles Lamb (1775–1834) looked towards the past, and nostalgia pervades most of his work. It was only in 1820, towards the end of his life, when the *London Magazine* was founded, that he became Elia and one of the

Charles Lamb, to whom we owe the *Essays of Elia*. From the painting by Hazlitt

most delectable English essayists. Yet, though Lamb's achievement was to lie just outside the Regency, one may briefly consider him here, for he was unconsciously preparing for it in Regency days.

He was born in the Inner Temple in 1775, the son of a scrivener. His early memories of the Temple, and of a family house, Mackery End in Hertfordshire, were to inspire some of his most charming essays. When he was seven and a half he went to Christ's Hospital; and, had it not been for his stutter, he might have gone to Cambridge and into the Church. As it was, he left school just before his fifteenth birthday, and in 1789 he became a clerk in the South Sea House. From 1792 he worked in the East India House, where he stayed for thirty-three years. He made his first appearances in print as a not-too-successful poet. In 1807 he and his sister, Mary, produced their *Tales from Shakespear*, a re-telling of the plays for children, and these came to enjoy enormous vogue.

Lamb was one of the most endearing English letter-writers. Humorous, witty, erudite and warm, his letters have an unmistakable style.

Thomas de Quincey, best known for his *Confessions of an English Opium-Eater*

I am going to eat Turbot, Turtle, Venison, marrow pudding – cold punch, claret, madeira, – at our annual feast at half-past four this day [he told Coleridge in 1814]. Mary has ordered the bolt to my bedroom door inside to be taken off, and a practicable latch to be put on, that I may not bar myself in and be suffocated by my neckcloth, so we have taken all precautions, three watchmen are engaged to carry the body upstairs – Pray for me.

The Essays of Elia were in a sense a development of Lamb's letters (more than once the same themes recur). The letters may explain why the essays have such a personal, intimate tone.

And here, perhaps, we should turn to another contributor to the *London Magazine*. Thomas de Quincey was born in Manchester in 1785; he hardly knew his father, a prosperous merchant who died when his son was seven. Thomas was brought up by his mother, who added "de" to the family name. He went to Manchester Grammar School, where he was kindly treated, but remained unhappy. After eighteen months, he ran away. He spent eight adventurous months in Wales and in London, which were crucial to his development. In

1803 he went to Worcester College, Oxford. He abandoned his poetical ambitions, and determined instead to become "the first founder of a true Philosophy". In March, 1804, he took opium to relieve facial neuralgia, and the initiation largely shaped his life. In 1813 he became a regular and confirmed opium-eater. He kept a decanter of laudanum by his elbow and steadily increased the dose. "A tedious proser though a sensible man," Crabb Robinson decided. "He wearies by the uniformity of his homilies."

In 1807 de Quincey had met Wordsworth and Coleridge. He had now become estranged from the Wordsworths, and married Margaret Simpson. But marriage did not bring him stability, and his financial affairs deteriorated. At last he wrote two articles called *Confessions of an English Opium-Eater*. They appeared in the *London Magazine* in 1821 and they were reprinted as a book the following year. Nearly forty years of life remained to him, and he wandered from friend to friend, and from lodging to lodging, fighting in vain against insolvency, until he died in 1859.

William Hazlitt (1778–1830) had a sharpness of intellect which both Lamb and de Quincey were denied. He was the son of a Unitarian minister. His early years were unsettled, as the family moved from place to place in search of a permanent home. In 1787, however, they moved to Wem, in Shropshire, and here he first had a proper home and a regular education. As his adolescence approached, he began to show his characteristic and resentful attitude to the world. His family intended him to be a Unitarian minister, like his father; but the training proved to be distasteful to him. He abandoned it, and turned to painting. In 1804 he first met Lamb, who remained an intimate friend until his death. Hazlitt's portrait of Lamb shows that he might have reached considerable distinction if he had chosen to remain an artist. At this point, however, he returned to his old enthusiasm for philosophy, and in 1805 he published his first book, *An Essay on the Principles of Human Action*. In 1813, at the age of thirty-five, he began the real work of his life: that of an essayist, journalist and critic. He soon came to be an influential critic of the theatre. In 1818 he published his collected criticisms under the title *View of the English Stage*. It is a comprehensive account of the theatre during the years 1813–18, the middle years of the Regency. Hazlitt concerned himself not only with the stage, but with politics, art and literature. In 1816–17 he wrote *Characters of Shakespear's Plays*, the first of his books to prove an immediate public success. In 1818 he published his *Lectures on the English Poets*.

William Hazlitt,
essayist and critic

It remains that I should say a few words of Mr Coleridge . . . I may say of him here, that he is the only person I ever knew who answered to the idea of a man of genius. He is the only person from whom I ever learnt anything. There is only one thing he could learn from me in return, but *that* he has not. He was the first poet I ever knew. His genius at that time had angelic wings, and fed on manna. He talked on for ever; and you wished him to talk on for ever. His thoughts did not seem to come with labour and effort; but as if borne on the gusts of genius, and as if the wings of his imagination lifted him from off his feet. His voice rolled on the ear like the pealing organ, and its sound alone was the music of thought. His mind was clothed with wings; and raised on them, he lifted philosophy to heaven. In his descriptions, you then saw the progress of human happiness and liberty in bright and never-ending succession, like the steps of Jacob's ladder, with airy shapes ascending and descending, and with the voice of God at the top of the ladder. And shall I, who heard him then, listen to him now? Not I! . . . That spell is broke; that time is gone for ever; that voice is heard no more: but still the recollection comes rushing by with thoughts of long-past years, and rings in my ears with never-dying sound.

In 1819, Hazlitt published his *English Comic Writers*. Some of his

131

best essays, on more general subjects, were collected in *Table Talk*, and the *Plain Speaker*; but these, his two most famous books, were published when the Regency was over.

The Regency was the age for critics. *The Times* itself earned the nickname of "the Thunderer", and expressed opinions with vehemence. *Blackwood's Magazine*, *The Edinburgh Review*, *The Quarterly Review*, and others, published criticism of a force and influence which can hardly be paralleled today. The Press was the only mass medium, and it therefore had all the more effect; those who wrote for it included men of intellectual power, and they wrote with conviction and style.

They did not simply devote themselves to criticism of the arts, they lent their power to social reform. One of the most effective reformers (and one of the most endearing men of his time) was Sydney Smith.

Born in 1771, he was educated at Winchester and Oxford, and he would have made a distinguished barrister. But his father had spent so much on his three other sons that Sydney had to choose the one profession that was open to a scholarly man with no private means. He entered the Church. He was ordained in 1794, and, after a few years as a country curate, he went to Edinburgh. His years north of the border were marked by two important events. One was his exceedingly happy marriage, and the other was the "bold and sagacious idea" which he put into practice with his friends Francis Jeffrey – the Father of Editors – and Henry Brougham, the barrister and politician. This was the founding of *The Edinburgh Review*.

The Edinburgh Review was indeed a daring venture, when one considers the state of England at the time. As Sydney pointed out:

The Catholics had not been emancipated. The Corporation and Test Acts had not been repealed . . . Prisoners tried for their lives could have no counsel; Lord Eldon and the Court of Chancery pressed heavily on the nation; libel was punished by the most brutal and vindictive imprisonments; the principles of political economy were little understood; the laws of debt and conspiracy were on a barbarous footing – the enormous wickedness of the Slave Trade was tolerated. A thousand evils were in existence, which the talents of good and able men have since removed; and these effects have been not a little assisted by the honest boldness of *The Edinburgh Review*.

When Sydney Smith associated himself with the *Review*, he knew that he was damaging his chances of preferment in the church; but, despite the dangers of liberalism, he continued to urge every kind of reform: colonial, educational, clerical and social. No contributor could claim and hold the reader like Sydney Smith. In one of his articles, he discussed a recent report on the need for climbing-boys: the wretched children who were forced up chimneys to clean them. The opening paragraph was a masterpiece of purposeful writing:

An excellent and well-arranged dinner is the most pleasing occurrence, and a great triumph of civilised life. It is not only the descending morsel, and the enveloping sauce, – but the rank, wealth, wit, and beauty which surround the meats – the learned management of light and heat – the silent and rapid services of the attendants – the smiling and sedulous host, proffering gusts and relishes – the exotic bottles - the embossed plate – the pleasant remarks – the handsome dresses – the cunning artifices in fruit and farina. The hour of dinner, in short, includes everything of sensual and intellectual gratification which a great nation glories in producing.

In the midst of all this, who knows that the kitchen chimney caught fire half an hour before dinner – and that a poor little wretch, of six or seven years old, was sent up in the midst of the flames to put it out?

Sydney Smith wrote for *The Edinburgh Review* for twenty-eight years. Even then, he did not say all that he could have wished.

In 1803 he had moved to London, and established himself as one of the wits and humorists of the age. He delighted the circle at Holland House, and reduced even Mrs Siddons to "a fearful paroxysm of laughter". In 1806 he was given a living in Yorkshire, in 1828 he was made a Canon at Bristol, and in 1831 – fifteen years before his death – he finally became a Resident Canon at St Paul's Cathedral. The Smith of Smiths had himself destroyed his chances of a mitre, but he had established himself as a Christian reformer.

Another reformer must be mentioned, though much of his activity lay outside the Regency years. This is the author, journalist and radical, William Cobbett (1763–1835). He was born at Farnham, in Surrey, the son of a small farmer. At the age of nineteen, he became a solicitor's clerk in London. Soon afterwards, he joined the army; he was drafted to Nova Scotia, and reached the rank of regimental sergeant-major. During his army days he also collected evidence of fraud and peculation. In 1791 he procured his discharge from the army, and demanded a court-martial of the officers involved. The court-martial was granted; but, in despair of getting a fair hearing,

William Cobbett

Cobbett fled to France, and later sailed to America. There he became a pamphleteer. When he returned to England in 1800, he was welcomed as a famous political journalist. From 1802 he was chiefly associated with the *Political Register*. He settled in the village of Botley, near Southampton, and brought a new note into radical agitation. But power had its penalties. In 1810 he was prosecuted for sedition, heavily fined, and sentenced to two years in Newgate. Here – for prison life was lax – he continued to edit the *Register*. When he was released in 1812 he appeared to be ruined, but he still had the *Register*, and in 1816 he began to issue a cheap *Register*, addressed especially to journeymen and labourers.

Friends and Fellow-Countrymen –

Whatever the pride of rank, of riches, or of scholarship, may have induced some men to believe or affect to believe, the real strength and all the resources of a country ever have sprung and ever must spring, from the *labour* of its people . . . Elegant dresses, superb furniture, stately buildings, fine roads and canals, fleet horses and carriages, numerous and stout ships, warehouses teeming with goods: all these are so many works of national wealth and resources. But all these spring from *labour*. Without the journeyman and the labourer none of them could exist; and without the assistance of their hands, the country would be a wilderness, hardly worth the notice of an invader . . .

Soon afterwards, in 1817, Lord Holland, the Whig peer, met this thundering reformer:

I saw Cobbett twice. His upright figure indicated the drill of a soldier, his ruddy complexion and homely accent the subsequent character of a farmer . . . Neither countenance nor conversation (at least of this time) were at all of a piece with the sprightliness of his style, the shrewdness of his remarks, or the closeness of his reasoning in written composition . . . He very unaffectedly acknowledged his distrust of his own nerves, and a dread of behaving meanly and basely if arrested; he, therefore, hinted at an intention, which he afterwards executed, of retiring to America.

It was this year that he went to the United States. Between 1817–19 he produced his *Journal of a Year's Residence in the United States of America*, and his famous *Grammar of the English Language*. In 1819 he returned to England as a leader of working-class agitation. From 1819–1832 his history is partly the history of the agitation for parliamentary reform; but Cobbett also found time for his other activities, especially his *Rural Rides* through the southern half of England. *Rural Rides* lie outside the Regency, but they show that Cobbett could express the hopes of a suffering class; and that, indeed, is the basis of his appeal.

The most vivid and authentic records of any age are the spontaneous, untrammelled comments of the men and women then alive. The Regency is often reflected in contemporary correspondence. Politics and life at Court are seen in the letters of the Regent, in those of Princess Charlotte, and in those of Mme de Lieven, the wife of the Russian Ambassador. Lady Bessborough records Society; Maria Edgeworth, bursting out of provincial existence in Ireland, covers the whole spectrum of English life in stylish, shrewd and animated letters. Charles Lamb talks of life and books in his archaic, personal manner, and Keats reveals the working of genius.

If the Regency produced many fine and illuminating letter-writers, it also produced a number of diarists of distinction. Among them was Henry Crabb Robinson. Born in 1775, he lived until 1867. Journalist and barrister, reformer, conversationalist, he was also the friend of many of the great men of his day. On 8th January, 1811, he began his diary: "Spent part of the evening with Charles Lamb (unwell) and his sister . . ." Thenceforward he kept a diligent and observant record of his friends, his travels and his reading, of politics and scientific invention. His diary remains an important source-book for the serious student of the age, especially for the student of literature.

There are, however, two diarists who remain apart. The first is Thomas Creevey (1768–1838). His parentage remains uncertain (he was possibly the natural son of a peer). Educated at Cambridge, he was called to the Bar. In 1802 he married a rich widow (and also became the Whig Member of Parliament for Thetford). His step-daughter, Bessy, later became his confidante and favourite corres-pondent, and it is said that his letters to her alone would fill the better part of a hundred volumes. The Creevey Papers include his diary as well as his correspondence. They present a vivid account of Pavilion life and (after the Regent fails to introduce a Whig govern-ment) they record bitter comments on "Prinny". Just before Waterloo, Creevey happened to find himself in Brussels; and so it was, a fortnight or so before the battle, that he came to meet the Duke of Wellington, and asked the question that posterity would have asked of him:

"And now then, will you let me ask you, Duke, what you think you will make of it?" He stopt, and said in the most natural manner: "By God! I think Blucher and myself can do the thing." . . . Then, seeing a private soldier of one of our infantry regiments enter the park, gaping about at the statues and images:—"There," he said, pointing at the soldier, "it all depends upon that article whether we do the business or not. Give me enough of it, and I am sure."

Creevey's account of Brussels at the time of Waterloo is a classic piece of journalism; and it was, inevitably, Creevey who hovered round the Duke's house in Brussels after the battle, and saw the Duke upstairs alone at his window.

Upon his recognising me, he immediately beckoned to me with his finger to come up.

. . . The first thing I did, of course, was to put out my hand and con-gratulate him upon his victory. He made a variety of observations in his short, natural, blunt way, but with the greatest gravity all the time, and without the least approach to anything like triumph or joy. – "It has been a damned serious business," he said. "Blucher and I have lost 30,000 men. It has been a damned nice thing – the nearest run thing you ever saw in your life . . ." Then he said: – "By God! I don't think it would have done if I had not been there."

This was not the only masterpiece of journalism in the Creevey Papers. The month after Princess Charlotte died, Mr Creevey discussed the problem of the succession with the Regent's brother, the Duke of Kent. If the Duke had sought a discreet adviser, a silent listener, he could hardly have found a man less to his purpose: Mr Creevey reported the conversation to the Duke of Wellington, and to Lord Sefton, who replied that "nothing could be more first-rate than the Royal Edward's ingenuousness". We may be grateful for the Duke's unwisdom and for Creevey's indiscretion. His notes of the interview were, it seems, written down immediately after the conversation; they are among the highlights of his Papers. In his letters and his diary, he continued to record momentous events until his death in 1838.

The Creevey Papers, as one might expect from a miscellany, are somewhat uneven in quality. They are remembered for notable chapters and occasional brilliant flashes, and for their cumulative effect. The political bias which gives an edge to Creevey's commentaries is also one of the weaknesses of the Papers. Such criticisms cannot be made of the Greville Memoirs. They cover a longer period and give a wider view of men and events. They form a continuous panorama; they are written by one man with more balance, style and dignity.

Charles Cavendish Fulke Greville was born in 1794. He came of one of the oldest families in the country, and his grandfather, the Duke of Portland, was twice Prime Minister. In 1801, when he was seven, Greville was appointed Secretary, in reversion, of the Island of Jamaica (in time, he duly came into his office, and made it a sinecure by appointing a deputy to perform his duties for him). In 1804, at the age of ten – again, no doubt, through his grandfather's influence – he was appointed Clerk Extraordinary to the Privy Council; he drew no salary, but he kept the right of succession as an ordinary Clerk when a vacancy occurred. In 1805, he went to Eton, and in 1810 he matriculated at Oxford. He went down in 1812, without taking his degree, in order to be private secretary to Earl Bathurst, the Secretary of State for War. In 1821 he finally took up his promised post as Clerk to the Privy Council; he held it for the next 38 years.

Greville began to keep his diary at the age of twenty, and his early entries record the defeat of Napoleon in 1814, his exile to Elba, and the quarrels at home between the Prince Regent and his wife and daughter. His accounts of the Royal Dukes and their wives are undoubtedly frank, and he cannot be said to ignore their weaknesses and eccentricities. It would be wrong, however, to assume that Greville's portraits are vehement, superficial caricatures. One of the qualities which strikes us most in his *Memoirs* is his power of analysis – a quality in which Creevey was deficient. Greville has a gift for cool dissection, for lucid, balanced presentation. He kept his diary until 1860, five years before his death. It shows the historian a superb sweep of history, from Napoleon's exile on Elba to the Crimean War and Garibaldi's conquest of southern Italy. It gives the literary chronicler an admirable collection of portraits. It is a massive source of documentation for the socially conscious. The Greville Memoirs are not just a source of documentation: their caustic, visual, highly personal style gives them a place in literature.

VII. THE REGENCY

SUCH WAS THE REGENCY. Its spirit and achievement continued through the reign of George IV. They ended almost with his death on 26th June, 1830. When the new President of the Royal Academy asked to attend the funeral of George IV, to show his colleagues' "grateful respect", he was refused permission, on the grounds that Benjamin West had not attended the funeral of George III. The Earl Marshal added, presumably as consolation, that the President of the Royal Society was also not entitled to attend. The reign of enlightenment was truly over.

The first public act of William IV, on the day of his accession, was to dismiss all George IV's French cooks. As Lord Ellenborough said: "He will have no foreigners about him." "His Majesty swears that nothing shall be encouraged but *native talent*," wrote Mrs Kemble, the actress, to her daughter. "The German Band is all disbanded," added Lady Williams Wynn to her son, "which Article alone cost £14,000 per ann. & throughout His Household he has dismissed every Foreigner." The late King's civilised tastes were discounted; so were his virtues. His subjects had not forgiven him for his extravagance, or for the disasters of his private life. They could not forget him soon enough. One of William IV's most popular gestures was made early in his reign: the famous cottage at Windsor was demolished. The Pavilion at Brighton was accepted, but in time it suffered its inevitable decline. William IV's successor, Queen Victoria, did not take kindly to it – and she had her own marine residence in the Isle of Wight. A Victorian critic dismissed the Pavilion as "a melancholy and ludicrous monument, resembling a group of tea-pots, candlesticks, and extinguishers". A visitor, wandering round Brighton in 1857, contrasted it sadly with the town of 1809:

How different is Brighton at the present moment, the Pavilion stripped of its gorgeous but fanciful furniture, has now degenerated into a public building – the scene of flower-shows and cheap promenade concerts.

The royal cortège has given way to flys and donkey carriages; and the statue of the Fourth George alone reminds the passer-by of the glories of that mighty magician, who, Aladdin-like, raised a magnificent town from a small insignificant fishing village.

The mighty magician, like his Pavilion, was to be abused; and as his friends and contemporaries died, as the Victorian ideal of bourgeois domesticity took hold, as the English puritan instinct reasserted itself, as the art of living became, somehow, equated with self-indulgence, George IV was sure to decline in favour. Much that Sir Thomas Lawrence painted, decided Fanny Kemble,

partook of the false and bad style which, from the deeper source of degraded morality, spread a taint over all matters of art and taste, under the vicious influence of the "first gentleman of Europe" . . . Hideous Chinese pagoda pavilions, with grotesque and monstrous decorations, barbarous alike in form and in colour; mean and ugly low-roomed royal palaces, without either magnificence or simplicity; military costumes, in which gold and silver lace were plastered together on the same uniform, testified to the perverted perception of beauty and fitness which presided in the court of George IV. Lawrence's own portrait of him . . . comes as near a caricature as a flattered likeness of the original (which was a caricature) dares to do. To have had to paint that was enough to have vulgarised any pencil.

Today, perhaps, we may question the value of contemporary doctrine. We may see the Prince Regent – George IV – as the most gifted man to rule England since Charles I. "Well may Prinney say as he does that 'he sees distinctly we are going to have Charles Ist's times again'." The remark, reported by Creevey, was eloquent. No King since Charles I had been so truly interested in the arts; and George IV showed a width and diversity of patronage, in music, painting and sculpture, the theatre and literature, medicine and science, which no English monarch has equalled.

Carlton House, is alas, his Nonesuch, long ago destroyed; but his Pavilion still proves his sense of fantasy, his romantic exuberance; and round the Pavilion, by his grace, hums the town of Brighton, which he created. Regent's Park, which his favourite architect designed, remains the most inspired example of town-planning in London.

If Buonaparte deserves the praise lavished so unsparingly upon him for his improvements of Paris, what praise [enquired a pamphleteer] can be too great for George IV for his improvements of London? A different city has arisen under his patriotism – a splendid capital, combining the glories of architectural cities, with the greatness of London and the domestic civilisation of England. His reign began in the triumph of arms – its conclusion was marked by the triumph of art. The arts have lost in him a liberal and discriminating patron.

Windsor Castle, which he altered with Wyatville, is very largely a monument to his taste; and Buckingham Palace bears his generous mark.

A man of extraordinary natural distinction, he drew men of distinction to him. He gave a heartwarming impetus to the art of living. That art has never been better practised in England than it was during his Regency, and his reign. The towns his architects designed, the houses that they built, the gardens and estates which surrounded them, reflected the natural taste of the time, unspoilt by commercial standards. Interior decoration, furniture and fashion had an elegance which we can only envy. If style and taste were the prerogatives of the upper classes, the humblest lived in surroundings of graceful simplicity, in a countryside which was still virtually unspoilt by the greed of speculators, the growth of industry, or the stupidity of ordinary men. Mass media – the Press apart – did not exist; there was no vulgar, communal and everyday entertainment to take the place of life and to blunt susceptibilities. Men and women depended on their own resources, they developed their own talents, they enjoyed simple pleasures, and they were, perhaps, more content with their lot than are their equivalents today.

Social injustice remained, but it was being remedied. Education was spreading, religion was an active force. In 1821, the year when the Regent was to be crowned as George IV, a clergyman declared from his pulpit at Colchester: "If righteousness exalt a nation, the means of righteousness abound. There is a growing attention to the education of our youth, and to the principles of our holy religion . . . Britain is presented before us in the present age, not merely as shining in arms, or as the emporium of wealth, but . . . as a dispenser of blessings to an impoverished and expecting world." In 1830, on the day of the funeral of George IV, another preacher declared: "He seized every opportunity of introducing and encouraging the arts of peace. The various public institutions of the country, for the promotion of religion and morality; for the relief of distress; and for the removal of disease; – and never were grander schemes devised for general good than in his reign: everything, in short, that tended to the welfare of the people whom he governed, received his prompt and permanent approval. Nor must the free profession of our holy religion, with all our other spiritual and civil privileges, be forgotten in our estimate of the late King's reign."

The Regency itself had been the dazzling age of Keats and Shelley, Byron and Jane Austen, of Turner, Constable and Blake, of Repton and Nash. It had been among the most brilliant ages in English history.

> Well mayst thou praise the land that gave thee birth,
> And bless the Fate which made that country thine;
> For of all ages and all parts of Earth,
> To chuse thy time and place did Fate allow,
> Wise choice would be this England and this Now.

So Robert Southey had written in *The Poet's Pilgrimage to Waterloo*; and many of his contemporaries would have agreed with him. The Regency had seen the triumphant end to the long Napoleonic Wars. It ushered in a century of peace which was broken only by the outbreak of the First World War in 1914. It established England as a world power.

INDEX